GOOD GUY
GONE BAD

GOOD GUY GONE BAD

Book 1

LAGANTRA OUTEN

To order additional copies of this book, contact:
Xlibris
1-888-795-4274
www.Xlibris.com
Orders@Xlibris.com
798434

Dedication

This is my first book and I am grateful to complete a novel, my first dedication goes to my one and only sister 'Elmira' may she rest in peace, she's been my inspiration since I could remember! My dedication also extend to my loving mother Pauline and my beautiful daughter Iesha, I love you both forever and ever!

CONTENTS

Introduction...ix

Acknowledgements...xi

Good Guy Gone Bad.. 1

Disappointment 3

Bernard 6

Starlette 10

The Family 12

The Phone Conversation 14

Starlette's Fantasy 15

The Visit...16

Nurse Parker 18

Gang Related... 20

Lagant meets Jada... 22

The Date 24

The Betrayal.. 26

The Deception... 28

Catch Up, Pay Up... 30

The Conversation 31

Miss Parker Flashback 33

Bubbles for Victoria...35

Fellas 36

Horny Thoughts 38

Shakur... 40

Victoria's Fantasy...41

Jada's Fears 43

The Amigo's.. 44

Beauty and the Beast 46

Victoria Calls it a Night 47

The Disguised Dealer 48

The Demise 49
The Land Cruiser Experience 51
The Mills Family 53
Inner Thoughts...57
Murder One... 59
Cotton Candy 61
The Flashback 63
The Home Coming.. 66
Itchy Feet.. 67
The Truth 69
Victoria's Dream Date 71
The Test.. 73
Shakur Meets Sis New Friend 78
Parkers Plot 82
Cotton Plays Chest....................................... 84
Professional Call 87
Fore Play 88
The Waiting Game.. 95
Sexual Healing... 97
Jada's Guilt..103
Khalil's Plan..105
Doggie Style..106
The Hit..108
Shakur Reprimand..110
Wee hours of the Morning 112
Another Day Another Dollar 119
Disappointment...121
Dirty Thoughts..122
The Tie In...123
Planting Seeds...147

Introduction

Paula was living in one of the hardest hoods, Newark, N.J., during the era of the two most treacherous gangs out. A single mother of three, she taught her children good standards and qualities of life. When tragedy struck their family she was able to keep a strong hold on her youngest son Lagant; for Bernard it was another story. Lagant didn't want to end up dead like his sister or in prison like his bro Bernard. To escape the dim light of Newark, of hood life, looking for a brighter future, he joined the Navy. There he meets Jada, the woman he thought was the love of his life, whom slowly tried to steal his youth. Until her secrets, lies and deceitful ways catch up with her.

Lagant discovered what he inherited from his unknown father, something which genetically flowed through his blood . . .

Being reunited with his older brother Bernard, who now goes by Khalil (changed his name in prison), Lagant is faced with decisions and situations that require a new perspective in life.

Acknowledgements

First, I'd like to thank the only one who is capable of bringing me forth out of the darkness and continuously enlightens me one day at a time; guiding me in a good, orderly direction; helping me to stay focused, appreciating my gift & more of myself; and learning what's greater! The One we all know and all need to love, the Most High, the All Mighty, the Creator of it all—without further ado—Father God (yes God has haters too)—that's sad and so not funny!!!!

Second, I'd like to thank the one person who has been by my side from day one, my mother! My words can't express my great appreciation and gratitude enough to you! You have been more than anything this world can offer! A Mother like you is very rare now days. May Father God and Mother Nature continue to bless you. I love you forever.

My first born daughter, Iesha, I love the way you grew up to be so beautiful; not only on the outside but on the inside. (A cup could be clean and shining on the outside with the inside being dirty & filthy; you can't drink from that cup). You are a cup of fresh air that is truly beautiful all the way around, inside and out. Keep up the good work and continue moving forward!! Daddy got you!! That's my Boo!! Tell your mother, Valerie, I said, "Job well done and I know no other woman could do the great job she has done!" To Ja'sya, my second calling, as longs as I have breath, we're going to get it right. Tell your mother, Catherine, to keep her head up.

To all my loved ones and friends who've moved on to a better place; you are not forgotten. RIP and please meet me at the cross roads. I need you to hold my hand again. RIP big sister Elmira—you might not be with us physically but in spirit we all feel your presence! RIP to my grandmother; Mama Cora, your life was not lived in vain, we all are holding on and going strong. RIP to my Aunt Beverly who taught me the meaning of being a Sagittarius. RIP to her daughter, Latesha Kim Mills, my little cousin whom always thought I was special. RIP to my Aunt Evelyn and her children who passed in the fire of love. RIP my cousin who took one for the team, Jerome Mills & son; the most thorough of them all!! RIP to the mother of the killa hood, Michele-aka—(Mama Killa) killa meaning: killing them with kindness, etc. RIP to my num#1 uncle Mr.Robert Mills 16 Nov.1937 layed to rest 27 July 2010, I always admire your strength, your presence would surely be missed! Those who RIP that I didn't mention, your passing is not forgotten!

Shout out to my brothers from another mother, Big Mel, Hykine Johnson, Ike, Cy, Skee, Slim-blood, Phil-Real, Federick Byrant, De'end Mccrae and his fam. My partner in the battle field, Keir Love; keep your head up! Don't ever let it fall. My cousins whom consider me the best—Cedrick, Arlinda, Pastor Margie Mills, Mr.Ron, Yolanda, Arnold, Fatima, Takisha, Love, Andrea, April, Dorothy, Nicole, Shakil, Jalisa, Raheem, 2-10—can't forget about my bro Sheek-Tarik/ Pablo from Littleton Ave community village. Good job on the book cover, created by: Samuel Lewis, you could get his information from the back cover! If I missed any one, my bad, the love is always there! I keep my circle tight!

Mad love goes out to my siblings and their children in order: my brother Ajamu, his wife Alice & their children, Quran, Sade and Lil Ajamu; my sister Shahidi and her children, Ashley, Nadiyah, Xavier; Nadiyah! I didn't forget how you put your two cents in when I was working on my book, I love you for that. Without y'all I wouldn't be the man I am today.

It wouldn't be right if I didn't shout out the people who helped me the most with the book; Bree, for typing and doing the first edit; Lateef, for doing the second editing and proof reading. Y'all help is greatly appreciated!!

Shout out to my Springfield Ave crew in Newark N.J.—bka—Springkill—aka—Da-Kill from Fairmont to Littleton. Wise Choice Clothing Store, Nubian Flavors Restaurant, Rock The Boat, if you ever in the neighborhood, YOU have to stop and check them out, it's great food and sports, urban clothes!! What up Mr. Charles thanks for your positive contribution to the hood! Big J, Big Chuck, Rell, Wan, Rashid, his wife Pam. I'm taking y'all advice, "I'm flying with the eagles and *leaving the turkeys behind." Now let's continue to make this money!!! What up Cousin Evelyn; what up to ALL my Killa's; what up Baby-Killa & J-killa, Diamond-killa; Wat up to my Ace! thanks Asia aka Voilet tell the rest of the Killa to stay strong!; Big Vee; to my Ninja 40, stay strong in the struggle tell the hommies behind the wall to never give up, like they told me "Anything could happen!" What up to ALL my ninjas on 006st Newark-AkA-Brick City!, ALL my SMM homies around the globe; to my cousins in the feds, Swift and Skillz; shout out to author Kareem Love for giving pointers. To my Facebook promoters, Monique Williams, Shanelle Bell, Tamara Left eye thanks for your dedication, patient and most of all your help; Big ups to my main man and 'em plus good friend's of mine Melvin Moore and Phoroah Mosbly: Mel for the support in KVK ent. And Phoroah for never stop believing in me since day one! Thanks for y'all help and being a friend. My shout out list can go on and on, if I missed anybody "wadup! Yall know how I do!!!"*

Oh I can't forget about my haters; it's too many to name but you know who you are. Too bad y'all fear what y'all don't know or understand! (Me!). That's because you never gave yourself a chance. I learned how to put my feet on top of your hate and let your hate raise me up. You dig me!!! (I'm surfing dude, I'm surfing on YOU!)

Good Guy Gone Bad

It all started to come to the light, after the birth of his first child whom he named Iesha, on one of the hottest summer days, July 24, 1992. It was one of the most important and best days of his life—up until the doctor congratulated him, after the delivery of his first child and said; "Now you have a pair, your son finally has a sister that he can play with." He stood there astounded.

Lagant is 22 years old and had been with the love of his life Jada for 3 years. Jada is 28 years old and the woman that he wanted to marry, age didn't matter to him when it came to love, it was just a number. They met on Lagant's 2nd tour in the U.S. Navy. Jada had kept the birth of her son a secret from Lagant so he was totally surprised by the doctor's admission. We all know. "What's done in the dark will soon come to light." But Jada had no idea that it would come to the light on the day that she gave birth to their first child. She had Lagant thinking that this was her first time ever bearing a child. Not only did she keep a secret, she also lied to him, but thanks to the doctor at Portsmouth Naval hospital her secret had been revealed. Now Lagant could see and learn more about her and her true colors.

Lagant was the type of young man who tried to do the right things in life, he was raised in a single parent home with his mother Paula and she did her best raising her family. Paula taught all of her children respect, honesty, and instilled good manners, standards and morals in them, in spite of living through the struggles and life tragedies that come along with being a single mother in the ghetto of Newark, N.J. Lagant was her youngest child of three. The oldest and her only daughter, Myra was the "It" girl that every man loved and wanted, and every female wanted to be like. She was very attractive and smart, the cream of the crop as some would say, she was just plain ole irresistible. Myra was in a committed relationship and she stayed loyal to her boyfriend, and this made a lot of men envious of her. So envious that one day her best friends' boyfriend tried to rape her! Myra fought for her life but he over powered her and strangled her to death in the process. The death of Myra devastated Paula and her family; she was only 20 years old when she was murdered. She left behind a 2 year old daughter by the name of Chantel. Lagant was only five years old, and his brother Bernard was ten and he took the death the worst. Bernard looked up to Myra they were very close; he was so over protective of her. With her being the oldest, he loved her like she was his mother. The day Myra was murdered Bernard vowed that one day he would revenge his sister's death.

After Myra's death Paula became protective of her children and tried to keep a close, tight net over them. It was easy for her with Lagant and her granddaughter Chantel, but Bernard was another story. He was old enough to understand the murder of his sister and it caused him to stop caring about quality of life and being good. In his eyes it was a reality check and he started running with a local gang in the hood called "The Lollypops"! And they welcomed him into their gang with open arms, they admired his courage and he received a lot of respect from the gang's leaders.

Bernard was big for his age; he was only ten but was built like a high school varsity football player. He was always in the streets, into one thing or another with his street gang, running 'round the city causing havoc. Bernard learned at an early age that life in the hood was a struggle; and he was determined to help his mother and protect his family. What his mom couldn't provide, he and The Lollypop's took. Paula had no control over Bernard, and Lagant felt like he'd lost the closest ones to him with his sister being murdered and his brother in the streets. Lagant believed that although his sister was gone, she left them the most precious part of herself for them to remember her by; her own flesh & bone, her daughter Chantel.

Disappointment . . .

Lagant kissed Iesha, his newborn daughter, and looked at Jada with pure disgust. His first thought to himself was to break up with her; he felt that he couldn't trust her anymore. She lied and had him fooled. He wondered if it was anything else she was hiding. Lagant was so upset and hurt, he didn't even say goodbye as he left the hospital. He was hurt that he had to find out such a serious matter, which should have been known to him a long time ago, in the privacy of their own home, from a doctor. Lagant was determined not to let the newly found bad news ruin one of the most important and special days of his life. Jada call out his named as he was leaving, he heard her but he ignored her and kept walking. He wasn't trying to hear anything she had to say. He wanted to stay optimistic about the situation so he went to celebrate the occasion by himself.

Lagant went to a pub in Norfolk, VA named The Moonlight Club; he sat at the bar and ordered a bottle of Moet with two glasses. The barmaid was gorgeous! Half Black, half Philippine, very exotic looking. Her eyes were a little slanted, with the cutest button nose; full lips that looked so succulent to him. She had the prettiest smile with teeth so white they sparkled every time she opened her mouth. She had a strawberry complexion with long silky black hair that hung down to the small of her back. Her body was out of this world! Curves everywhere and anywhere you could imagine. She was definitely a diva that hadn't been discovered.

Lagant was mesmerized by her appearance; he couldn't keep his eyes off her. He had to concentrate just to keep from staring at her. There were 3 other guys sitting at the bar, all trying to impress her. 2 of them she knew by name; the third guy was very persistent. every chance he got—he tried to get her attention. He was buying shot after shot, and after every shot he'd offer to buy her one; but she kept declining. She was very respectful and courteous to everyone who sat at the bar, the pub was empty but Lagant noticed a flyer that read, free drinks for all ladies from 9pm to 10pm. So he knew it would soon be packed with lots of women. The barmaid brought over his bottle of Moet in a fancy metal ice bucket with the 2 champagne glasses and asked, out of curiosity, "Who's the other glass for?" Lagant replied, "For any nice lady who cares to celebrate with me tonight." She smiled and said. "I like celebrations what are we celebrating?" Lagant answered, "The birth of my daughter, and the break up with her mother!" The barmaid looked confused and said, "Oh, I'm glad and sorry to hear that." Then she introduced herself. "My name is Starlette, my friends call me Star, and it looks like you can use a friend." Lagant smiled and said, "My name is Lagant, but my friends call me Gant and yes you're right I could use a friend." Star smiled and replied, "I get off in ten minutes, and I'll celebrate with you if you'd like?" Starlette liked Lagant. She saw when he first walked into the bar wearing his Navy whites. She thought he was very handsome and sexy in uniform. And she loved his dark smooth skin, his bedroom eyes, and his sexy ass lips.

Lagant is 5'11, 200 pounds with a stocky build, and kept a clean shave with a light mustache. He wore his hair styled in what you call a low faded Brooklyn cut. Starlette liked his style; he wasn't like the other guys who frequent the Moonlight. every other guy tried their hardest to get her attention and ask her out, but she knew they were just trying to get into her pants. Her older brother always warned her about those types of men.

Starlette thought to herself his baby mother is very unfortunate. She pushed her thoughts aside and said. "I'll see you in ten minutes, that's if you accept my invitation?" Lagant smiled and said, "Yes I'd be delighted." Lagant let Starlette know that he was moving the celebration to one of the cozy tables in the back; and she told him she'd meet him there. While he was waiting for his new friend to return, he thought of how Jada played on his intelligence and led him on for three years. Which she made HeLL, drama after drama. Now he was ready to catch up on all that he had missed out on and see how she feels when the tables are turned. He thought about how beautiful Starlette was. He couldn't believe that a "top model" barmaid chose him out of all the other guys who tried to push up on her. As Starlette was walking to join him, he noticed how fierce her walk was. Her hips swayed from side to side just like she was on a runway, modeling. She wore an all red matching outfit that was spandex; it hugged as if it was her birthday suit! Her pants were low rise; with a short sleeve v-neck that showed her cleavage! It was just long enough to expose her flat stomach, with a gold belly ring that had a diamond stem with a heart hanging from it. She wore an anklet with a heart medallion with a pair of red stilettos, and she had a matching diamond bracelet and necklace with heart medallions. Lagant stood up as she approached and pulled out a chair for her. He was trying to be the perfect gentlemen. As she bent over to sit down he glanced at her butt and thought, "damn! This girl has the full package, she's heaven sent, flawless!" Automatically he fell in lust.

Bernard

By the age of 20, Bernard caught an attempted murder charge on a foe gang member from The Avenues. The member had disrespected his baby's mother, and besides that, The Avenues were getting beside themselves lately. They thought because they were in large numbers, they could go into other hoods and do what they wanted to do. They were from up the hill in the west ward in Newark, and The Lollypops were from the same ward but down the hill. The two gangs were natural enemies in the 80's, The Avenues would try to come into The Lollypop's hood when the Lollypops was around and try to rob, steal cars, and talk to their girls. When the girls didn't give them any play they would start disrespecting them calling them Lollypop suckers and throw rocks, or even shoot in the air to scare them.

When Bernard caught up with the guy who disrespected his baby mother Alice, he hit him across the head with the butt of his 9mm and the guy took off running for his life. Bernard fired 3 shots,—POP-POP—POP—The first bullet hit him in his left leg causing him to fall; the second bullet missed his head by inches. Bernard ran up on him, and stood over him looked him in the eyes and said, "suck on this you bitch ass nigga!" He aimed at his head, he heard the police sirens coming. He still pulled the trigger but the bullet missed the deadly head shot, and it hit the guy in the shoulder. Bernard took off running but with him being so tall and big it was very easy for the witnesses to point him out. The judge sentenced Bernard to 10 years in state prison.

Bernard was being released on parole after serving 7 years. He was lucky to be released on his first parole date. He used his mother's address for parole. She was so happy to know that her eldest son was coming home. She hoped that prison helped him grow into manhood, not knowing that prison made him more dangerous than ever before. With his not giving a fuck attitude in prison, he had to fight almost all the time. Other gang members always seemed to test his gangster because he was a big young boy from the Lollypops.

The Lollypops were small in number but their hearts were as big as a lion's. They all stuck together and were down for whatever, whenever and they never took anything lightly. In prison Bernard became a Muslim and changed his name legally to Khalil, he felt that it fit his personality; the Arabic meaning is close comrade/friend. Khalil's motto was if you're a close friend he'd ride & die with you. He held his spot down in prison, he wasn't the leader but he made it to second in command. There were only 5 other Lollypops in Rahway prison. There was Rashad, who was the one who introduced Khalil to the Lollypops when they were just kids. Rashad was fourteen, young and dangerous; he robbed everything moving, and had no problem shooting anyone who wasn't connected to his hood.

Then there was Dick-Dick that now goes by the name of Big-D, he was always the fastest in everything; stealing cars, breaking into houses, and fighting. His fist were fast like lightning, he could hit a dude 10 times before they even could blink once. He gave himself the name Dick-Dick because he said that he had fucked the most girls in the hood. His motto was dick'em down and be on to the next one. His fellow gang members called him Dick-Dick because he could never get caught by the cop, he ran so fast that everyone would say, "Damn, you see how fast he dicked them!"

There was Rock, he was just a ruthless motherfucker, and every crime that he had something to do with was always left bloody and grimy. Rock was only called on when it was time to put in bloody work and the most serious matters, because he would go so over board. His name fit him so well as a young Lollypop; he had a small body with a big ass rock head. One day when he was younger they were outside play fighting Rock trip and hit his head hard on the curve; everybody stopped and asked if he was ok. He just got up rubbing the spot on his head and shook it off like nothing ever happened. He yelled out, "I'm good." And started right back playing everybody thought his head was really a rock. He was known for taking the most pain, it seemed like nothing ever hurt him. One day when he was around fifteen he got hit by a speeding car while running away from a robbery; he wasn't looking as he ran into the street on Littleton Avenue. The impact from the car flipped him; he hit his head and rolled 5 times and jumped straight up and started back running like nothing ever happened.

7

When everybody made it back to the hide-away they asked him, how he survived that hit. But on the other hand this is Rock.

They were all fortunate to be down state with their leader, Charlie Brown. He started the gang when he was fourteen years old; he was known for being the brains behind everything. He was very street smart with a brave heart. Some wondered how he was able to organize a street gang at such a young age, the word was that his father gave him all the information and strategy he needed from inside the pen. His father was doing a life bid in prison for triple murder. No one actually knew Charlie Brown's real name, and they wonder why he wanted to go by that name, but they all respected it. Charlie Brown was known throughout the hood and the city of Newark, along with his gang.

Once there was a grown man named Numbers, he was well known in the hood for being a gambler, and he took Charlie Brown & the Lollypops as a joke. He thought since he had seen these little knuckle heads growing up and knew their parents that he could disrespect them. One night he decided to try the gang calling them Charlie Brown and his suckers, Numbers was going back and forth making jokes. His last joke was the old song, "Charlie Brown—he's a clown." While Numbers was pointing and laughing at Charlie Brown, Charlie Brown took the chain that he had around his waist and wrapped it around his fist, sucker punched Numbers in his temple, knocking him out cold. Then he took the chain and strangled him half to death. Numbers is paralyzed on one side of his body till this day.

The Lollypop headquarters was in building 54 on 16th Avenue, everyone already knew not to bring any trouble around there. That's where Charlie Brown lived and also sold his drug's and guns. The building was a four story building with eight apartments, four on each side. At the age of sixteen Charlie Brown moved out of his mother's apartment; {she lived on the left side on the second floor of the building} into the first floor apartment. The police didn't have a clue that illegal activities were going on, they figured it was a bunch of teenagers playing outside instead of a ruthless goon squad that they really were.

The Lollypops would give cookouts in the summer for the whole neighborhood; they would help the less fortunate with food, clothes and with the children's school supplies. All the neighbors loved them because of their support and the protection they gave in the hood. They were a close knit street family, and would recruit females into the gang.

The females were called the Lollypoppette's, or Poppette's for short, and they were true riders.

Charlie Brown or Cool Breeze as he goes by now, stands at 5'10, 170 pounds; he had been down state for 5 years. He caught a first degree aggravated assault charge. He got caught fucking the leader of the Avenue's girlfriend. Cool Breeze was in their apartment when Alimean came home and heard his girl screaming out, "I love this lollypop." She was licking and slurping all over him. Cool Breeze followed saying, "Lick It like it's your favorite lollypop—oh—bitch—I'm about to fill your mouth with the cream filling." Alimean tried to open the door but the lock chain was on the door, he quickly kicked down the door and ran into the front room and saw his girlfriend slurping on Cool Breeze's dick! He got so furious, he bum rushed Cool Breeze; Cool Breeze was caught off guard with his pants down. They struggled but Alimean wasn't strong or fast enough. Cool Breeze fucked Alimean up so bad; he had to get reconstructive surgery on the left side of his face, leaving him blind in the left eye for life. Alimean cooperated with the police.

Starlette

Lagant and Star enjoyed their night celebrating his awkward occasion; he began to make small talk. "Star where is your man?" "I'm single, but I'm accepting applications." They both smiled and Lagant continued, "A gorgeous lady such as yourself, working in a nice club like this, I know you have many men that offer to take you out." "Yes but I really don't find any of them interesting; they offer but I decline. They all are mostly regulars who come in here to see who they can catch for a night; I've seen it all in the year I've worked here." She smiled then said, "But I've never seen someone like you come in here with a Navy uniform on and order a bottle with two glasses, and sit by his self." They both shared a laugh while he poured more of the Moet into their glasses, and made a toast. "Here's to meeting two stars in one day, first my daughter Iesha now you Starlette. May God add a blessing on this special day!" They bumped glasses and sipped on their Moet.

Starlette was 25 years old, she had moved from California where she was born and raised, to Virginia Beach a year ago. Her father was in the Navy, and had retired as a captain. She moved to VA to help out with her brother's businesses. She asked, "You must be proud of the Navy coming in here with your uniform on?" He paused and looked across the room then at himself in uniform and said, "Usually I would of went home and changed, I was feeling a certain way so I didn't care—and just came in here. Don't get it fucked up I got swag and could get jiggy with it!" Star just listened and smiled while they became more acquainted with one another. The other guys in the club were looking at Lagant with envy in their eyes, but he didn't pay the haters any mind. He was from Newark, NJ, one of the hardest hoods in America, so he wasn't worried or afraid. They started to feel good off the Moet; he offered to drive her home. "Are you able to drive home?" She laughed and said, "Gant we didn't drink nothing—I can hang with the night dogs, like Patron, Dom-P, Remy & Mr. Hennessy! Remember, I'm a bartender! I can get it in and hold it down!" "Oh you talking slick, I'm going to hold you to your word." When the bottle was finish and the night was getting later. He looked her in the eyes and said, "I enjoyed myself, thanks for celebrating with me—I really needed your company. I like our new friendship—can we do it again sometime?" She smiled showing off her pearly whites, waving her finger, and then said. "Of course, don't tell me you thought you were going to get away with out keeping in contact with me?" He smiled and yelled out jokingly and said, "Oh no! I already have my number written down for you." She smiled as they exchanged numbers. He walked her to her car while she told him how much she enjoyed herself just talking with him. He wanted to kiss her but he was a little shy, and didn't want to move too fast and scare the diva off.

As they approached her car, he noticed the brand new, all white, German paint styled, 92 Lexus coupe; with light tint sitting on chrome 22 inch spinner's, low profile Pirelli tires. She leaned over and gave him a kiss then slid her tongue into his mouth giving him a passionate kiss. Lagant was surprised but happy that she kissed him first. He grabbed her by the waist and firmly pressed her exotic body close to his and returned the passion. Their kiss seemed like the 4th of July, they smiled and looked into each other's eyes; you could tell what they both where thinking . . . "Good night Star." "Don't say good night yet, wait until I get home and call me." "I'll call you and wish you more than a good night." He stood there as she smiled and pulled off; he looked up to the sky and said, "Thank you God!" He felt Starlette had to be a gift from the heavens above.

The Family

Paula prepared Bernard's old room; she knew that he changed his name to Khalil but she didn't care, she was going to call him by the name she gave him. She cooked a special meal to welcome him back, his favorite; T-bone steak, fresh steamed collard greens, bake potatoes, and homemade butter milk biscuit with her extra sweet kool-aid. All of the immediate family was there besides Lagant. Chantel now has a 1 year old daughter named Ashley; this was his first time meeting his great niece in person. She was the prettiest, with a light brown complexion, and chubby cheeks. He couldn't stop hugging and kissing her. After dinner Paula called Lagant, "Hello son, I have a surprise for you!" When she said surprise he realized that his brother must have came home. He cut his mother off and said, "I have a surprise for you too!" Paula screamed out, "Don't tell me Jada had the baby!" "Yes she was born on the twenty-forth." He knew his mother would have a lot more questions for him; like why she wasn't the first to know; he really didn't feel like going into detail. He knew it would only lead back to the upsetting news he had received from the doctor. "They're still in the hospital—I was on my way to visit them when you called— but let me speak to my brother!" "Ok—but how you know that was my surprise?" "I knew it wasn't a million bucks (he chuckled); I knew it was around this time that he was coming home." "Call me back when you get back from the hospital, love you son." "I love you to mom!" "Gant what's up Navy boy?" "everything gravy!" "Now you don't have to visit big bro in prison anymore!—A nigga free! — when you bringing your family up?" Khalil had so much to say that he didn't even give his little brother a chance to reply. "How does it feel being a father?" {Nonchalantly} "It feels good—and I'll try to get up there when my daughter gets around six months—when she can handle the ride." Khalil asked, "Are they still in the hospital?" "Yeah—I was on the way to see them now—I know you feel good being home again—bro do me a favor and stay the hell home—we need you home not in the cage!" "You know it—I'm not trying to go back to prison!—Look bro, I'll holla at you, go and visit your little one and tell Jada I said congratulations!" "I'll make sure." "Handle your business— one." "You right, I'm out bro—peace."

The Phone Conversation

It was eleven o'clock pm when Lagant call Star; he kept his word. Star left no leaf unturned; their conversation was so intense and deep; they both felt comfortable getting more personal over the phone. It was feeling like they knew each other long before tonight. Lagant was talking a lot of bedroom sweet talk, and she was loving every bit of it; smiling ear to ear, laughing and blushing. She didn't want to sound desperate or seem easy, but she told herself if he asks to come over, "I'm going to let him." She felt herself getting wet in between her thighs, she loved his voice, and she kept picturing him in her mind. Star was overwhelmed with their phone sex conversation. She had to change the subject before she got too weak and invited him over. "What took you so long to call me? You had me waiting a whole twenty minutes!" Her question broke Lagant's spell that he was trying to put on her; he thought to himself that his charm just wasn't working, he had been out of the dating game far too long; he hoped that she would of invite him over. He was laid back on his queen size bed, palming his dick, imagining having sex with the Moonlight's diva! "Only if he knew all he had to do was ask!" Lagant answered, "I was giving you time to get comfortable and settle in—that's all." "Don't let it take you that long again", she said jokingly. He replied, "It's not going to happen again baby." Star started making small talk officially ending their phone sex and crushing any dreams of him getting in her bed tonight.

They had so much in common. Lagant started to become restless, so he told Star goodnight and said he wished their date will have them walking on the moon, amongst the stars!" "I already see us there together." They both smiled and said their goodnights with Star blowing a kiss threw the phone. "I'll talk to you tomorrow."

Starlette's Fantasy

   Starlette laid back on her queen size bed after the sensual phone conversation, and started to think about how they met and how much she enjoyed his company. She started to reminisce on their phone sex, and she pictured him walking in her bedroom getting into bed with her. Her imagination started to run wild, she began to feel his hands massaging her body, along with his lips kissing all over her breasts and sucking on her nipples. She was laid back with her eyes closed, caressing her body, making her desire rise even more. She started moaning and calling out Lagant's name; her nipples were extremely hard and her pussy was tingling. She imagine him taking off her black lace thongs and bury himself deep, deep inside of her, she took her two fingers, wet them with her mouth and began to rub her clit and sticking her fingers in and out of her already wet—hot pussy. She imagined Lagant's long stroke inside of her, putting her legs over his shoulders and gazing into his eyes. Star began to lose control, gyrating both her nipples and clit. She felt like she was in heaven; the last time she had sex was over 2 years ago and now her whole body was shivering. She was moaning uncontrollably as she stroked her pussy faster and faster until she felt fire spark in her spirit. She screamed out Lagant's name over and over as she had the orgasm of her lifetime. She gripped the satin sheets pulling them into a ball, both legs shaking with her ass cheeks tight her hips lifted up off the bed. Breathing hard, her pussy juices poured out into her hand onto the bed, it felt so warm coming out in squirts. After her orgasm was over she thought to herself, "Damn, Lagant! You're what dreams are made of! If I feel this way by just masturbating, I can't wait for the real thing!" She went to sleep with Lagant on her mind.

The Visit

Lagant arrived at Portsmouth Naval Hospital the following day around 7pm; his new born daughter was in the room with her mother. Jada was happy but nervous to see him, so she spoke softly, asking him how was his day and she'd hoped that he wasn't to upset about what he heard the doctor said. She felt bad that she had him believed Iesha was her first and only child, and that he had to find out by her doctor that she had a son; she knew he wasn't beat to hear anything she had to say. Lagant was only there to visit his daughter; she was so pretty; being born premature didn't mean anything as long she was healthy. He called her his little star. In spite of the bad news he learned about Jada, he remained polite and answered her questions, keeping it short and simple. He took a seat in a chair and watched as she continued to feed Iesha. "Did you call and tell your mom that I had the baby?" Jada asked, and he answered. "She just called me before I left the house—I told her and I spoke with my brother—he's home from prison." "Khalil finally made it home, that's good news, I know he's happy." Jada wondered if he told his family about her other child. Lagant could tell that she went into a deep thought by the way she paused; he assumed she was wondering if he had told her secret. He waited while she came back from her inner thoughts; her eyes dropped 'n what looked like a bit of sadness filled them. She knew she owed him an explanation but she didn't know where to start; so she figured she would wait for him to ask. She did take notice of his attitude change; he hadn't hugged or kissed her, no flowers or balloons. She finished feeding Iesha, burped and cleaned her up then asked Lagant if he wanted to hold his daughter. He grabbed the blanket and placed Iesha into it and picked her up. She looked into his eyes like she knew who he was. She smiled and he smiled back saying, "that's my boo; how's daddy little girl? You know I love you!" Iesha smiled the whole time; he gently placed kisses all over her pretty little face. Jada tried to make small talk while he walked around the room, but he wasn't trying to hear anything Jada was talking about, he felt she needed to come correct with him. The nurse entered the room breaking the tension. She was a good looking white lady in her late thirties with a name tag on that read Parker. She spoke to Jada then asked, "How's the happy family doing?" "everything's fine." Jada replied. Miss Parker quickly took notice that it wasn't such a happy atmosphere, so she remained professional and told Jada that they would be releasing her tomorrow between 8 or 9 am, and to make sure that she had a car seat. Lagant spoke up telling Miss Parker, "I'm the father I will pick them up tomorrow and I'll have the car seat." "Okay." Then she turned to Jada and said. "I'll see you next feeding then." Lagant watched as Miss Parker walked out of the room, and thought to his self, "Damn she has a phat ass, she looks sexy as hell in her nurse's uniform." He imagined sexing her on one of the hospital's beds; she was very attractive with a shaped like Serena Williams, she had hazel eyes with long black hair that she wore pulled back in a bun. After he finished watching Miss Parker his attention went right back on his daughter. It was getting late so he decided to head home; he didn't want to call Star too late, plus he was hoping on seeing her tonight. He told Jada that he would be there in the morning to pick them up, kissed his little angel and told her. "Daddy loves you." Jada asked for a kiss but he paid her no attention as he walked out of the room. She called his name over, and over as he walked down the hall.

Nurse Parker

As he waited for the elevator, he couldn't stop thinking of Star; he figured he'd call her from his cell phone in hopes of setting up a date. He thought to himself. "There are a lot of pretty women in the world; Star must be one of God's special, advanced additions of women. Damn! she so gorgeous!" As the elevator door opened Miss Parker was getting off, she spoke to Lagant and asked, "Leaving already?" Lagant eyes became wide. "Yes—I'm going home to get some rest so I can be here early to pick up my little one." "Congratulations on your baby girl, (She knew it was now or never.) May I ask you a question and hopefully I'm not being too personal."

It depends on your question." "Is Jada your wife or just your baby's mother?" Miss Parker had a flirting twinkle in her eyes as she asked hoping he'd say what she wanted to hear. Lagant knew she was interested in him by the question, so he extended his hand and properly introduced himself to her. "That's a unique name I've never heard it before its gentle yet masculine." "Are you flirting with me Miss Parker?" "Only if I can!" He asked her for a pen and wrote his number down along with a note that said, "I can't wait to hear from you." He passed the pad back to her and continued. "She's just my baby's mother; call me anytime after 5 pm." "I most certainly will!" He stepped on the elevator and pushed for the lobby floor; while Miss Parker stared at him, they both smiled and winked their eyes, as the elevator doors closed. Miss Parker thought to herself, "Damn Lagant is fine, how could Jada let him slip through her hands, he'll be mines soon!"

Miss Parker knew that she had to have him when she saw him in Jada's room. For the first time in her life, she wanted to give a strange man her cookies. She loved how his body was structured, his walk and stance, and how his voice sounded when he spoke, he was just right for her. His presence sent chills down her spine; she pictured hugging and kissing him. Miss Parker didn't want to disrespect Jada openly, so she keep it professional in the room, but it was another story and perfect timing that they ran into each other at the elevator.

Miss Parker was divorced for over 15 years, and the last relationship she had only lasted six months and that was more than five years ago. She had been dedicated to her job; it helped her fill that empty void in her life. Now she was ready to fill that void another way. Lagant not realizing, they both were thinking the same thing, SeX!

Gang Related

When Khalil's homeboy's found out he was home they all gave him the traditional welcome home ceremony, and all the original Lollypop's were there, besides Cool Breeze. They gave him all he would need to get his life started on the streets again; cash, pounds of marijuana, a 38 special snub nose. They took him around the hood and introduced him to the new recruited family. They explained that the Lollypop's had changed their name to The Fellows; that stood for {Forever Living Large out Witting Society and for short Fellas; Forever Loyal Living as Soldier}. COOL BReeZe changed the name because when they were in prison the soldiers became reckless, and the FeDS were on their ass trying to build up a racketeering case but they never could figure out who was running the gang. everybody in the hood was calling themselves a Lollypop and wearing shirts with the gangs name and a red charms pop on it. So with the name change other gangs didn't know what to think, they thought The Fellows where a new gang that teamed up with the Pops so they stayed clear. The Fellows were now the most dangerous gang in Newark.

As they rode threw the different hoods Khalil saw his son Qu'ran chilling with some of his hommies; Qu'ran wasn't in a gang but he was affiliated by the reputation of his father. Khalil didn't want his son in a gang, living a life of crime. He felt like he had joined to make a better way for his family. He tried to be a good father but being in prison for so long, Qu'ran wasn't used to having a father figure around. They pulled up to Qu'ran, five cars deep and jumped out saying what's popping and peacing each other. Qu'ran spotted his father, and was amazed at how much respect his father had in the hood; he wanted to be just like his father, he also knew his father didn't want him hanging around with the little Knights; this was the name for the up and coming Fellows.

Khalil wanted to spazz out on his son but he remained calm, he didn't want to embarrass him. He told him to get into the suburban. Qu'ran wasn't planning on joining; he knew his mother wasn't having it. He was smart in school and very respectful to his teachers; he knew one day he wanted to play professional football. Qu'ran didn't think he was doing anything wrong by hanging out with his crew; he was too young to realize or know the hidden dangers that came with hanging or being in a gang.

Lagant meets Jada

Lagant got off the elevator feeling like God's gift to women, first Star then Miss Parker and they were both official. As he got into his car his thoughts were about Jada. He felt hurt by her secret, his feelings were still strong towards her; they had been together for 3 years. He thought about when they first meet on the USS Yellowstone. Jada was already stationed there for 2 years when he checked on board. He had no idea there were so many beautiful women in the Navy; it was so much going on that he didn't notice Jada. Once he settled and the work day was over, it was liberty call for all the sailors who didn't have duty. The ship was docked in Greece; Lagant and his friend Lester, whom he had met in the Navy academy school, both checked on the ship together. They became close from being in the same classes together; Lester was 28 years old and Lagant was 19 years old but very mature for his age. Lester liked the good energy of life that Lagant possessed; he also admired how the women took to Lagant.

Jada spotted Lagant the first day he checked on board the ship; she knew she had to have him. She went to get dressed and over heard the other females all talking about the new meat that checked on board. They all were talking about Lagant until Jada stepped in and said, "I'm letting you all know right now!—the brown skin one belongs to me, so don't try me!" She pulled rank, claiming Lagant while not even knowing him. The other women fell back and just watched; they didn't want any problems with Jada; they knew she would make work hard for them in the future.

Jada was good looking about 5'7 in height and 130 pounds with a nice shape and curves in the right places. She was a light brown complexion and wore her hair like Halle Berry. She was 25 years old and experienced, she won Lagant over by using her wisdom on him. She knew exactly what to do and how to charm the young lamb into her waiting arms. Lagant loved how kind, nice, and generous she was; she made him feel like "the man". After all these years he realizes it was all apart of her plan to catch and trap him.

The Date

It was 8:30 pm when Lagant called Star. She picked up on the first ring. "Hi-Gant!" "What's up my Star?" "Thinking about you; hoping that we can do dinner tonight, I get off in thirty minutes." "Are you cooking?" "No silly, but I know this nice restaurant outside the Hampton's on the dock, they have the best seafood. Do you like seafood?" "I love seafood!" "Can you meet me at my job at nine?" "I sure can, I'll be there." "Ok handsome." "See you at nine beautiful." Star was happy that he accepted her invitation, she thought of the passionate night she dreamed about the other night.

Lagant realized that he was moving kind of fast, starting something new and not actually ending it with Jada. He had told Star that he was celebrating the break up with his baby's mother on one hand, and then on the other hand Star knew they were still living together. Lagant summed it up; if she doesn't mine, it don't matter, she older than me, she knows what the fuck is going on. He smiled and thought, "There's nothing wrong with friends with benefits." He was already dressed for the occasion with a burgundy Coogi sweater, a pair of beige Polo pants. With the dark burgundy mauri's, with his diamond cut chain that hung to the bottom of his chest that had an L medallion attached. He splashed on Polo sport cologne and headed his gold, sports coupe, five speed Acura to the Moonlight. He arrived at the Moonlight five minutes early; he knew Virginia like the back of his hand. Being from the hood he made it his business to learn his surroundings, one of his favorite sayings was, "You can take the man out the hood, but you can't take the hood out of the man." He could drive his 5 speed sports coupe swift like he was a NASCAR racer. He circled the parking lot twice looking for Starlette's Lexus, he wanted to park beside her. He couldn't find it so he gave up and double parked by the entrance and waited for her to come out. Star walked out smiling from ear to ear looking directly into Lagant's eyes. Lagant reached over and push the passenger door open for her; every guy out front was trying to get Stars attention. She ignored every guy as she got into the car and said, "Hello Chocolate." He blushed with shyness and said, "How you gorgeous." She gave him a kiss then told him to drive around back to where she was parked. "I've seen some Lexus's but they don't compare to yours." Star laughed and said, "I didn't drive my car. I drove my truck the Land Cruiser, the burgundy one right there. Same color you have on." His eyes became wide, "Damn! That's your Land Cruiser?! I need to work at the Moonlight, tips must be good." She smiled and gave him a flirting pinch on the cheek and said, "Park your car we're taking the cruiser!" He parked his car and as they were walking to the cruiser she threw him the keys and said, "These are the keys to my heart I want you to drive." Lagant caught the keys with one hand smiled and said. "You givin' me the key to your heart?" "Do you think you can handle it, protect it, cherish it, and promise not to break it?" "I will protect you & this key as I protect my own life!" "It's too early to tell." "I know when to stop at a red light, yield at a yellow, and pass on green." "For now were going to put it on the yellow light." "I feel you! I appreciate the fact that you trust me enough with the key!"

They continued to flirt and share laughs all the way to the Hamptons. They were listening to Al Green's greatest hits CD, they were singing along with the songs, especially Love & Happiness; they repeated that song the most. They arrived at the restaurant Seafood Delights; it was a nice romantic spot that sat on the dock overlooking the Atlantic Ocean. The restaurant was spacious with a 50 gallon fish tank with the most exotic salt water fish inside with a large wicker castle. There was another fish tank that had the lobsters, and another just for the crabs. Lagant was impressed at Star's choice for their first dinner date.

The Betrayal

Jada sat up as she rocked her new born baby girl to sleep; she had a lot on her mind. She knew she had to come straight and be truthful with Lagant. But it was hard for her, she was a young teenage girl at the time and to bring back up something that she dreaded would bring back all the memories that she hid for so long.

Jada grew up in upstate New York in a small family; just her mother and older brother William. Jada was close with her father, and felt that her mother made him leave them, driving him away with her evil ways. Her mother Bernadette was mean and strict; it was either her way are no way. When their father left he moved to Connecticut, he would call and send money to them, but Jada missed his presence. William mostly stayed in the streets, only coming home to eat, sleep, and shit. Bernadette used to scream at William about his ways, saying, he was never going to amount to anything just like his father. William always knew she was the reason their father left and as soon as he got old enough he was leaving too.

No one knew Jada was pregnant; she had fallen into the arms of a slick talking, young Mack. She thought he was attractive, she loved that he was understanding and always listened to her problems. Jada thought that she was in love; she would meet him every day after school at their friend's garage, they had set it up as the hang out spot. She would go home after school and do all of her chores and homework. Then she'd ask her mother could she visit her girlfriend. Her mother didn't mind as long as she got home before dark, her mother didn't have any idea that Jada was going to meet Henry.

Henry was in his early twenties, and had a main girlfriend that Jada knew nothing about. She thought she was his only girlfriend not knowing that she was only his side piece. Henry wanted Jada because she was a virgin. When she first found out she was pregnant, she was happy, but afraid of what her mother would do to her. She kept hearing her mother's evil voice repeat over in her head, "I will kill you and that baby if you ever try to bring a baby in my house!" Jada was frightened to death. After the second month, she brought another pregnancy test, just to make sure the first one was correct. She thought Henry would be ecstatic when she told him the news. She went, like always, to meet him at the garage. She told him, then pulled out the pregnancy test and showed him. She hugged him and said; "Baby, we can get married now!" Henry stood there with the most distorted of faces. She asked him if he was okay; he straightened out his face and pretended to be excited; he hugged her then told her he would support her in any way that he could. Jada was happy and thought that everything would be alright. The next day she wanted to tell her mother, but she thought about it and became scared, again. She figured that she would wait until Henry married her, then she could tell her mother. When she went to meet Henry like always before, he wasn't anywhere to be found; never again!

The Deception

Jada's thoughts were interrupted when the nurse entered the room to do her last rounds. "Hello Miss Parker." The nurse spoke as she marked on her chart, "Hello, are you ready to go home tomorrow? I see Iesha is sleeping comfortably." "Yes, she was ready for nighty night; I fed her, burped her and changed her pamper". Miss Parker knew she had a little time to try and get the most information about Lagant that she could from Jada without her becoming suspicious. "I see you have support from you husband?" "Yes—but unfortunately were not married." "Oh, I'm sorry, don't worry he will ask you soon—now that you two have a beautiful daughter." Jada looked off in a quick daze; she knew her relationship was on the rocks. She needed to vent to someone, why not her nurse, she felt that Miss Parker was very professional and that she could confide in her. "I don't know— I haven't been to honest with him—I don't think he trusts me anymore, but I really love him and I don't want to lose him—I was wrong for building our relationship on dishonesty, I didn't mean to—I figured I had to persuade him into liking me—Now we have a child together and I don't know what to do—he is younger than me and I don't think he's ready for marriage, at least not with me." Jada shook her head as tears fell from her eyes. The nurse replied, "You never know what could happen, just give him a chance, he'll come around." "I hope so he's only 22 and I think he has some more exploring to do in life before he's ready to settle completely down. But I know he will provide for his daughter—He has already made her a crib, and tattooed her name on his arm inside of a heart. "Do you two live together?" "Yes." She paused then looked to the ceiling to hold back her tears from falling. "I don't know for how much longer—though." Tears poured from her eyes as she continued to express her deepest feelings.

Miss Parker handed Jada some tissue. "I don't know what I'm going to do!" "everything will work out; for now—you just get some rest, you're a mother now and your daughter is going to need you!" "You're right, thank you for listening Miss Parker." "Goodnight Miss Jada Willis." Miss Parker walked out of the room with more information than she expected. She felt bad for Jada only for a second, and then she thought to herself, "Hey you win some, and you lose some; and if Jada doesn't step up, she just lost one!"

Catch Up, Pay Up

Paula was concerned with her oldest son Benard/Khalil, he didn't come around to her house after his welcome back home feast, and he never reported to parole. His parole officer had called the house and told Paula that he had missed all his appointments. He explained that if Khalil doesn't report into his office the next day, he will be forced to put a warrant out for his arrest. He didn't want to do it but at the same time he wasn't going to lose his job for an ex-convict. Khalil visited his parole officer the first day he was home and got the instructions, but honestly he wasn't beat. He didn't think it was fair that he had to be monitored, he quickly developed an I don't give a fuck attitude and made his mind up that he would pay up when they catch up with him. He was already smoking weed and running the streets like he was never on parole. Paula called Alice's, his baby's mother, house to relay the message, but he wasn't there.

The Conversation

As Star and Lagant sat on the dock waiting for their food to be served, she asked, "How does it feel being a father?" "It feels good, I always wanted a family—I wanted all my children to by one woman—but I see that's not going to happen—Life is full of surprises." "Do you think you will ever get back with your baby's mother?" Lagant sat back in the chair, took a drink of red wine and thought to himself, "She's really digging deep trying to feel where she fits in with me." Lagant sighed and said, "To be honest with you Star, I still love her for having my baby but I don't have feelings for her anymore. I've been feeling this way for awhile now, I tried to make things work for the sake of the baby but sometimes you have to ask yourself—What love got to do with it?" He took another sip of wine and continued, "She makes me feel like I don't exist—but it seems like things got worse!" Star continued to sip on her wine while she listened to him; she could hear in his voice and see in his eyes that he was serious. She wanted to know how he felt about a relationship with her; she knew it was too soon to put another commitment on him, so she kept it at the (yellow light). She had a lot of questions on her mind, and felt like tonight was the perfect night to get them off her chest. "Do you have any other women that you're interested in?" Lagant laughed. "I'm serious, why are you laughing?" "Besides you?" "Yes—besides me!" Lagant looked at Star's eyes rolling and necking rotating. She said, "Well I'm waiting! And don't lie to me Gant!" Lagant smiled and said, "There's a female lieutenant that works in the personal office name Miss Washington. I had a crush on her—but she doesn't know I had eyes for her—I keep it professional." "Keep it like that!" He put his hands on Star's and said, "Since I met you I haven't seen anyone more attractive than you— you've been kind, sweet and very understanding to me—But, I have a question for you Star—For the life of me I can't figure out what makes you interested in me?" Star smiled and placed her hands on his cheeks, and looked him in his eyes and said, "I don't really know what it is about you, but I've never felt this way for any man in my life. It's something about you that makes me feel so good on the inside—from the first time I saw you . . ." "I understand your situation and I appreciate your honesty—I ask that you always keep it real with me. I don't want any problems with no other bitches! I deal with one man—when I'm interested, it's all about him—and I'm interested in you! So don't act up— and when the time is right we can step it up, but for now I don't have any problem with being your friend." Lagant smiled from ear to ear, and said. "With benefits?" Star smile and gave him a love tap on his cheek.

Miss Parker Flashback

Miss Parker arrived at home after work at 10 pm. She lives in the wooded section of Newport News. She has a huge 5 bedroom, brick house with a 2 car garage. She has a pit-bull named Bones. The judge in her divorce awarded her the house from her husband, who is a doctor. Victoria Parker had been a nurse for fifteen years; she is the head RN in charge of the prenatal department. She has one daughter that is in her freshman year at Harvard University, studying for her law degree. After her divorce, she devoted all of her time to her daughter and job, going on dates throughout the years, but never finding someone to fulfill her very special needs. Most of the men she dated were either doctors or lawyers and didn't have the time for the attention she was looking for. She had a bad experience with her husband who never had time for her; only the other females' nurses and women. She knew he was cheating but the last straw was when she came home early from work hoping she could surprise him on his day off. When she made it home, there was another car parked in her spot. She thought maybe her husband had one of his golf buddies over or something. Once she entered the house, she saw a Louis Vuitton bag in the living room, a pair of grey stilettos on the floor, and a bottle of Grey Goose with two glasses, one of which had red lipstick on it. Music was coming from their bedroom; she put her work bag down and crept up the stairs making her way to their bedroom. As she got closer, she could hear moaning and heavy breathing. She stood in front of the opened door and couldn't believe what she was looking at. It was the shock of her life; she stood there watching her husband fucking some strange women in their own bed. Frasier was standing up with his back to the door giving it to the woman from behind; she could hear him saying. "I'm about to explode baby cakes— You ready for it Kera?" "Give it to me doc." As Frasier and Kera finished enjoying their orgasm, he told her, "You keep giving it to me like that your going to make me leave my wife!" As he turned around to pick up his pants, he saw his wife staring at him with an unbelievable look on her face that quickly turned into anger. All Victoria could say was, "Frasier—she already did!" She turned around and ran down the stairs and out the door, got into her car and left; with Frasier trying to catch up with her while trying to put his pants on at the same time.

Bubbles for Victoria

Victoria was quickly met by her dog Bones when she opened the door, he was always happy to see her. Bones would hear her car pull up and run to the front door to greet her. She loved Bones since a puppy; she returned the love and then let him outside for awhile. She would usually take a shower then be off to bed but tonight she was in the mood for a hot bubble bath. She figured she'd celebrate her catch of the day, (Lagant), she couldn't get him off of her mind since meeting him earlier today. She wanted to relax and get her thoughts together; she grabbed a bottle of Cristal and poured herself a drink then took the bottle with her into the bathroom which was located in her master bedroom. She turned the water on and poured in a cap full of Calgon vanilla scented bubble bath. Victoria walked back in her bedroom to get undressed; she turned her uniform to the back and unzipped it then slid out of it like a snake sliding out of its on skin. She wore an all black matching lace bra and panty set; she was a curvy woman that would have given the Cowboys' cheerleaders a run for their money. She sipped on her champagne then grabbed her silk robe and headed back into the bathroom and lit a vanilla scented Glade candle. She hung her robe on the door—hook and unbuttoned her bra; her titties looked like the perfect pair of firm melons. She slid out of her panties exposing her bikini wax, and then gently laid her beautiful body into the bath.

Fellas

Cool Breeze finally caught up with Khalil, he bought a bottle of Remy, a pound of purple haze weed, and a Sprint cell phone. He gave them all to Khalil then asked, "Can you smoke, or is parole on your ass." Cool Breeze wanted to smoke and celebrate their freedom, while they caught up on things. "Fuck parole! I've been smoking from day one, my parole officer called my mom's house but I've been staying with my baby mother. I'll pay up when they catch up! And if I really want to get low, I'll go to Virginia and stay with my brother. So fuck it—roll that shit up, I smoke up until I choke up, feel me!" They both laughed and Khalil opened the bottle of Remy and took a swallow. "Damn!" Kahlil said, as the Remy was burning his throat. "I forgot your brother is in the Navy. So he's station in Virginia? That's the spot to be, I heard it's a lot of money down there." "Yeah, he's down there cooling, he just had a little baby girl. I need to see my niece anyway, plus I know there are a lot of bad bitches down there on the beach!" Cool Breeze changed the subject and began to tell Khalil what was going on in the hood. "There are no beefs; in the hood every gang is bowing down to us; so basically, we run Newark, Irvington, parts of east Orange and Orange! We have money coming in from every direction; the soldiers are holding it down. Since I've been home they hit me off with $50,000; you know we go by the Fellows now? It's a new chapter! We on our grown man shit now, feel me." "Yeah bro, I've been informed— you know my little son run with the Knights right— I told him to fall back. I already made a path for him, with the game being so deep and everybody knowing he's my son, he gets the respect. I know he can hold his own but I don't want him to get trapped up in the things we use to do, feel me!" "Yeah, I know your little man, he reminds me of you but a little calmer.

I've seen your little man in action; he'll fuck somebody up then yell out, "Who else wants some of me!" "And trust—nobody answered him! I don't know Khalil; I think your little man wants to pop off!" They both laughed, and Cool Breeze continued, "Look my nigga, I don't want you to worry about money; take this $20,000 and my favorite hand, bitch, my 40 cal. Be safe, but focus on getting right with your family—you've been locked up seven years straight. Take this time and shake the prison dust off your ass! Cool Breeze took a pull of the haze then passed the dutch to Khalil as they continued talking about what was going on.

Horny Thoughts

Lagant looked at Star and said, "It's so beautiful out here I can't ask for anything more; the stars are so beautiful in the dark blue sky. The moon is full and the ocean sounds like soft music, but the best thing of them all—I'm with the most beautiful Star there is—you—You shine so bright, you light up the night; you're the only Star I see that's right!" He smiled at her to see how much she liked his just made up poem. She was smiling from ear to ear, "That was so sweet Gant, do you mean it?" Star was thinking about the ride over to the restaurant, and how much fun they had singing together. She loved how he made her feel so comfortable with him; the waiter interrupted their conversation with dinner. "Can I be of any more assistance?" Star answered, "Yes, can you please bring us two coronas, one with lemon and the other with a lime." The food smelled and looked so delicious, Lagant didn't waste any time eating, he asked Star if she wanted to try his fish. "Yes—and you try some of my garlic shrimp—open wide." She picked up the juicy garlic shrimp and placed it in his mouth; he ate the shrimp and licked Star's fingers at the same time. "Umm, I like the shrimp, but your fingers taste better!" She was surprised that he licked her fingers, but she liked it, it sent chills through her body. The whole atmosphere was perfect, very romantic and sensual; Star was feeling the effects from the red wine. Lagant noticed that her nipples were protruding through her blouse. She was looking sexy in her low cut green blouse, with a black mini skirt that showed her smooth reddish legs. He didn't want to stare but every chance he could get he dropped his eyes to sneak a peek.

They continued eating and flirting, their minds were on sex but they kept it to their imaginations. They could feel the sex in the air; he was sitting across from her with a hard-on stronger than Hercules and Iron Man put together. every chance he got he would slide his hand between his legs to push his manhood down, so it wouldn't bust through his Polo slacks. every time he looked at Star he would undress her with his eyes. Star couldn't take her eyes off of his lips; she liked how full his lips were, and imagined kissing them. She imagined him kissing all over her body, mostly her hot spot. Her panties were so wet; it felt like her pussy was in a pool. The waiter brought the bill and sat it on their table and collected their plates. "Hope you enjoyed your meals, please come again." Lagant reached for the bill, but Star grabbed it and said. "Gant I got the bill." "Don't make me feel bad Star, I am the man." "Gant get with the times, a female can pay! Besides, I invited you to dinner." He smiled and said, "Your right." She gave him a kiss and then excused herself and went to the rest room to wipe her juices off. Lagant walked over to the rail on the dock over looking the Ocean, and watched as the wave's moved back and forth. He was trying to control himself; everything seemed to remind him of making love to Starlette.

Shakur

Shakur pulled his van into the garage around 10:30 pm; he had just returned from South Carolina meeting his cocaine connects. Shakur is a very smart man with two legit businesses, besides his hustle. He lived in Chesapeake, V.A with his family, and stayed off the radar. He owned the night club called The Moonlight, and a painting & plumbing business in Portsmouth named P&P other than his hustle. He used his P&P utility van to make all his drug pick-ups and drop-offs. He had four employee's working at P&P and two other vans that all looked alike with the same color and company's advertisement on both sides. His workers didn't have any idea of his side hustle or his night club, and he didn't operate on cell phones when it came to his side hustle. He moved very strategically. All orders must go through the club as a work order; he had a hand full of customers that he dealt with. His sister, Starlette, handled all the calls and orders for his side hustle through the club, and his customers knew to speak with her between 12pm thru 9pm. If they missed calling her within the designated time they already knew not to call until the next day. Starlette would place the orders on Shakur's desk in their own personal codes. Shakur taught Starlette everything she needed to know, he also assured her that nothing would ever come back to her if things ever went wrong. He paid her very well for her services; she got paid on the books for being the clubs manager, and he paid her once a month for the side hustle. Shakur was already a millionaire and he didn't have to hustle; it had taken him time to get to his level; and he wasn't planning on giving up on his side hustle while the money was flowing like water. He'd been lucky thus far, no cops, no FeDS, no enemies.

Victoria's Fantasy

Victoria took a sip of her champagne, and let her imagination run wild. The bubble bath was helping her relax; it was so hot & soothing, she felt she was in paradise. She contemplated on how she was going to get Lagant. First thing was to get Jada off of his mind; she felt a little bad knowing that Jada wanted to work things out with him. But she figured she was tired of being the good girl and if the roles were reversed, she felt the next girl would've done it to her. She poured her third glass and pushed Jada out of her mind and started fantasies about Lagant. As her thoughts became deeper, her hormones started to flare up and she could feel her pussy tingling. She was determined to get a piece of him, she could tell that he could fuck by the way he walked, with his bow-legs. She started rubbing the soap on her breast; her nipples were one of her hot spots. She rubbed them in a circular motion and watched as they became erect; she took her right hand and slowly palmed her pussy while massaging it up and down. She laid back in the tub and placed one leg up on the top of the tub, while playing with her pussy and pinching her nipples; and with the other hand she extended her middle finger inside of her pussy and rubbed her clit with her thumb; it felt so good playing with herself while thinking of Lagant. Her legs were jerking every time she hit her g-spot. Without even realizing, she slid two fingers inside of her stroking faster and faster. Her moans were getting louder as she pictured Lagant fucking her. She wanted it harder, she took her hand and started gyrating her clit firmly; she was about to lose it! Water and bubbles was slashing everywhere. While screaming "yes!" in intervals, she placed three fingers inside her, pushing them faster than before, and as hard as she could go! Seconds later, she orgasmed screaming Lagant's name, with her body jerking like she got shot with an AK-47. Her body was so tense; she started shaking while saying, "oh-oh-ooow" while her juices continuously flowed. She was stuck in a trance!

Jada's Fears

Jada tossed and turned all through the night. Her thoughts went back to when she was giving birth to her daughter. She was happy to have a healthy, pretty little princess, whom she would protect from any harm. She knew that no one would take her baby away from her this time. She was happy that Lagant was there for the birth, she didn't have any idea that the doctor would assume that he was the father of her son, or mention it at all. She thought of the confused look that was on Lagant's face when the doctor congratulated him on having a son and a daughter. She knew he had questions, but wondered why he had not asked her about the situation yet. She knew that she had to explain things to him. She loved him with all of her heart but she was afraid he wouldn't understand and leave her. It was hard for Jada to trust men after her son's father, Henry; hurt and played her out by disappearing after she told him she was pregnant; leaving her a young pregnant teenager with false hopes, to defend on her own. She thought all men were alike; but being that Lagant was young, she felt he was innocent and she could use him to put trust back into her life. But not realizing; hiding her pass built up some kind of dark revenging demon insider of her. She reminisced about all the good times they shared overseas. All the beautiful countries they visited, the walks they use to take holding hands talking about everything under the sun. Lagant was very understanding, so Jada knew keeping it from him was a mistake. He had shared all of his deepest darkest secrets with her and most of all, his trust. She put her thoughts aside and tried to get her mind right; she was so emotionally scarred; she knew the trust he had in her would diminish once she told him the whole truth.

The Amigo's

Khalil passed Cool Breeze the Dutch. He continued to tell Khalil everything that he needed to know. "One last thing, Rock was suppose to come home on parole next month, he was doing good until this Puerto Rican nigga named Loco from the Amigo's. You've heard of them crazy motherfuckers from over in North Newark?" Loco was down for an attempted murder; Rock didn't know Loco but when he spotted Rock on the tier, he had flashbacks. Loco got a banger from one of his fellow Amigo's. It was well crafted, it looked like a real dagger, with both sides of the blades coming to a sharp point; the blade was six inches long with a cardboard handle holding it together. Once recreation time was over, Loco was in his bunk laid back, searching his mind trying to remember exactly where he knew Rock's face from when it finally hit him. That's the nigga that robbed and paralyzed his Amigo, Solo!

Rock and two other Lollypops went on a robbing spree in North Newark back in the day. Loco was in the store, while Solo and Marco were out front hustling. When they robbed them it was so fast and slick you couldn't tell there was a robbery in process until the shots popped off; and by then it was too late. Loco remembered the night clearly and could see Rock putting the gun to Solo's back and shooting him, pushing his body forward causing him to fall face down in the dirt. Marco was in shock, he was only 15yrs old and had never been in a situation like this before; he figured he was next, that's when he fainted.

Rock was on his bullshit that night; he was upset that all they got that night was $500.00 and a 007 style 9mm. Before he pulled the trigger, in a harsh voice he said, "Ya'll been out here all motherfucking day and this all you bitches got?!"

From that day on Loco never forgot Rock's face; now he was down state on the same tier with him. Loco knew he had the drop on Rock.

Rock didn't have any idea who he was; it had been over 4 years since the robbery, and he had never even seen Loco before seeing him in prison. Loco was plotting; thinking of the best way to take Rock out without getting caught. There was no doubt he was going to get revenge for his Amigo!

Beauty and the Beast

Lagant and Star left the Seafood Delight walking hand in hand to her Land Cruiser. Lagant was being the perfect gentleman; he opened the door for her and closed it behind her. He got in the Cruiser wishing it was his, turned down the radio and let Star know how much he enjoyed himself and thanked her for the meal. She smiled and said, "No problem, you're very much welcomed, I enjoyed myself also." He turned up the radio and started rapping to Big Daddy Kane's "I Get the Job Done." Heading back to Norfolk, Star played with his hair and massaged his shoulders the whole ride back to the Moonlight. Lagant rubbed her legs and enjoyed how smooth they were; he took his chances and rubbed his hand across her hot spot and felt the warmth coming from the middle; she grabbed his hand and said, "Yellow light!" Then Star crossed her legs so he couldn't sneak another touch; but she continued to rub on his legs teasing him. As they pulled into the club parking lot, the security guard waved and looked surprised as they passed, he never saw a guy driving her truck before. They stayed in the truck talking and flirting, neither of them wanting the night to end. She wanted to ask him to stay the night but didn't want to get rejected. Lagant knew he had to get up early in the morning, but in his mind he wanted to make the night super "star" special. He tried to break the sexual tension in the air, "Damn, I wish I didn't have to get up so early tomorrow." "I wish you didn't either." "The night is still young, and I don't want it to end." Star leaned over and gave him the kiss of a lifetime, long and passionate, and then she started rubbing his manhood. Lagant grabbed the back of her head their tongues were licking, sucking and working like two vampires thirsting for blood. Star continued rubbing him in hopes of bringing the beast out, beauty was now ready to meet the beast.

Victoria Calls it a Night

Victoria had masturbated so good she didn't want to get out of the tub, she was so relaxed. She hadn't been with a man in 2 years, she was practicing celibacy. But lately she'd been feeling that her clock was ticking out, and had been craving a man's touch badly. She finally mustered up enough energy to lift up out of the tub and give herself a quick shower. She let the water run down her body then dried off and put on her silk robe. She was drained from all the fantasizing. She went to her bedroom and laid on her king size water bed, then turned on her 36 inch plasma to watch a little CNN. She loved watching the news, and was up on all the worldly events; she was very intelligent and experienced in life. But she'd never experienced a black man and was anxious to find out if the myths were true: "Black men's cocks are long like a donkey's; the darker the berry the sweeter the juice; and once you go black you never look back!"

The Disguised Dealer

Shakur quickly unloaded 20 gallons of paint, which was really 20 keys of cocaine, and stashed all but 2 into the underground floor safe. The safe was professionally built and was designed not to show the opening in the floor. To the naked eye it looked like a normal floor. It was accessed by a button that was extremely hard to find; only he knew where the button was located. All of his neighbors thought he was a single guy and worked at P&P; he stayed ten steps ahead of the game. He was cool with his neighbors, they would refer their friends to his P&P business; they never suspected him to be a big time drug dealer nor a millionaire. To everyone he was the average working man; making an honest living. He never showed off, he only drove his work van to his stash house. Shakur broke down the 20 keys and packaged them in the correct weight amount for his buyers. everything was perfect, packaged in 10 gallon paint buckets, sealed up and ready for delivery. His basement was his work shop; it had all sorts of tools and equipment required for his businesses. Both of his businesses were legit, tax paying jobs but his side hustle money was all his; none of which went to those fat, back stabbing, greedy people that worked at the IRS in which he felt.

The Demise

The next morning Loco got up for breakfast and tucked his banger into his sock, and stood in the back of the chow line. He searched for his enemy; Rock was already sitting down eating with Rashad and Big-D. The Amigos had already told Loco about all the other gang members on the tier. He knew they were all from the Lollypop's, but he didn't care. He figured he'd catch Rock when he was by himself so there wouldn't be anytime for his boys to help him. Loco knew exactly how the system worked, he knew the guards would be on the scene after to take him to lock up but he didn't care as long as his mission was accomplished. Loco figured after breakfast was over would be the perfect time for the hit. With it being so busy, the guards couldn't pay attention to everything that was going on. Loco didn't eat breakfast he just got a cup of milk then went back to his cell so he could spy on Rock. He planned to run up on Rock in his cell and catch him off guard. He spotted Rock and his crew leaving the mess hall. He saw when Rock peace Rashad; Rashad had morning classes learning masonry. Big-D asked Rock again, to come outside and workout with him. He was trying to get Rock to workout with him since they were eating breakfast, but Rock kept declining saying he was going to take a shower and fall back in his cell. All Rock was thinking about was his parole date that was coming up. He was preparing his mind for going home, living with his mother and taking care of her. Rock walked to his cell to gather his things for his shower. Loco crept up to his cell. "Can I borrow an ink pen?" Rock looked at Loco, and thought to himself. "Who is this little motherfucker?" While thinking at the same time; why didn't he ask one of his Spanish friends? "Sorry my friend, I just need it to fill out the visiting form, I don't want any trouble—I'll give it right back." Rock laughed to himself at his accent, and Loco figured that he had won his trust for the moment. "Hold on—I got one—you could have it." Loco eased in and slid the blade out from his sleeve gripping it tight in his hand, as Rock turned around he charged him stabbing him in the shoulder. "What the fuck!" Rock screamed, "This is for my Amigo, Solo, nigga!" Rock did the only thing that he could do at the moment and that was to stick the pen straight in Loco's neck hitting him in the juggler. "Nigga this is for you!" Loco was shocked; he didn't anticipate getting stabbed, he thought it was going to be an easy hit. He stumbled backwards while pulling the pen out of his neck, and gave Rock a look as to say, "Nigga you killed me!" Blood was squirting out of his neck like water from a busted pipe.

The Land Cruiser Experience

Star reached over and reclined the seat back as far as it could go, she had a treat in mind for Lagant. She unbuttoned his pants, and slowly pulled his beast from his boxers. She loved what she saw. She was holding it in her hands and thought to herself, "Damn it's nice, long, fat, and it curves to the right, wow!" She looked in his face and noticed how he was enjoying the attention she was giving him. Lagant was lying back hoping that she'd do more than just stoke it. Then out of know where she placed her warm, wet mouth on the head of the beast and it sent chills through his body. He was shocked that she was giving him head in her truck, but was happy to help her christen it. She had his eyes rolling to the back of his head, and he was biting down on his bottom lip at the same time saying, "It feels so good baby!" That gave her more courage to get freakier, and she opened up showing him more of her best skills. He was ready to fuck; he tried to maneuver to switch positions but she pushed him back down and told him to relax; he couldn't control himself any longer. He started breathing so heavy, he couldn't warn her as he released his seed into her mouth; his hip sprung upward, he grabbed the back of her head and was saying her name as she swallowed. She wanted to give him a treat but she wasn't planning on swallowing. This was her first time but she liked it. "You're the best!" He wanted to return the favor, he elevated her legs over his shoulders and slid her black lace panties off and saw her neatly shaved spot. He became even more excited and erect again, he took his fingers and opened her pussy lips exposing her clitoris and thought he was in heaven. He licked and sucked all on her like it was his last meal. She was enjoying every second of him eating her out; she leaned back while rubbing her hands through his hair. She was moaning his name and telling him he was doing it just right; he was driving her crazy with his tongue. He wanted to bury himself deep inside of her; they didn't have a condom but was caught in the heat of the moment. They looked into each other eyes as if saying it was on, and started kissing uncontrollably as he inserted his penis deep inside of her. They started fucking like maniacs. They had the Land Cruiser bouncing like it had hydraulics.

The Mills Family

{Our Father who art in Heaven, hollowed be Thy name, Thy kingdom come, Thy will be done on earth as it is in Heaven. Give us this day our daily bread, and forgive us for out trespasses as we forgive those who trespass against us, Lead us not into temptation but deliver us from evil, for Thine is the kingdom, the power and the glory, forever and ever, Amen— Lord God! I kneel down, coming into Your presence humbly asking for forgiveness— Begging You to have mercy on our souls—all my family from the youngest to the oldest—the weakest to the strongest—protect us from all harm and danger that we can and cannot see—Help us rise above negativity and lead us to Your pasture—keep us on the straight and narrow path—Let none go astray for Your names sake—Father God I pray to You in the name of my Lord and Savior, Jesus Christ, Amen.} This was the prayer that Mrs. Paula Mills prayed for her family just before she prepared herself for bed every night. Paula had a big family that originated in Georgia and branched off into several parts of Florida, with her moving up to Newark, NJ in her late teens. She married her first born child's father, Ben, who was a little older than her, but loved the ground she walked on. Ben joined the Army to support his new family. He was a good father and husband that provided for them, but that didn't compare to his presence being missed. Paula gave her first born Myra everything she wanted plus more; she was determined to give her the things she never had growing up as a child. Myra was never spoiled by the things her mom gave her. The most important thing to Myra was the comfort and love from her father that she was missing. Paula's second born Bernard was eleven years later, and after his birth, her marriage started to get rocky. Paula was faithful but Ben wasn't, he became an alcoholic and a terrible cheater. The Army had changed him so much; she tried to save their marriage but couldn't stand to put up with his adulterous ways; she decided to separate from him and moved on with her life. The only money she had coming in was from her home seamstress business that she had started after Myra was born. She had loyal cliental that was constantly growing; everybody loved her work and would refer her to friends and family. Ben only came around on the kids birthdays and holidays to treat them for the occasion. The kids still loved him but felt that he gave up on them for another woman. Paula was finished with men in her eyes, but her sisters always told her not to give up on love. They reminded her that Ben was her first love but not her last and that it was his lost not hers. They were very supportive and they encouraged her daily. She was still young and beautiful, and had men inquiring about her all the time. Her sisters begged her to go out with them for a night on the town and she finally agreed. She made them the best looking gowns in the city for that night. When they arrived at Club Zanzibar, they lit the club up, all heads turned to their direction. The D.J gave them their due respect, by lowering the music and saying. "Ladies and gentlemen allow me to introduce you to Newark's finest three stars!" All the men started clapping and shouting, even some of the females. The sisters were treated like royalty. The club invited them into the VIP section, and everything was on the house. Paula was having a great time, she hadn't been out in a long time; she loved catching up on all the fun that she had been missing. After that night, Paula was back into the swing of things. When Ben, her ex-husband, got word that she was the hottest single woman back on the dating scene, he became jealous. He went to her house drunk demanding her back, but it was too late, Paula was completely over him. She was now dating a man named Homer that she met one day coming from the grocery store with her kids. Homer saw her come out the store and pulled up on her in his 1965 money green Cadillac, riding slowly, asking her if he could give them a ride. She said no thanks that they could manage. She only lived down the street, but Homer was persistent, he continued to talk to her while following her closely. He tried to flirt without being disrespectful to her children. Once she got home she said, it was nice meeting you and goodbye. He quickly parked, jumped out the car and asked, if he could see her again. While replying that she would think about it, she closed the door. He stood there thinking, I'm not going to give up—she too fine a lady. He knew it was hard to find women like her. The next day he was out in front of her apartment with flowers, blowing the horn and calling her name. She looked out the window and yelled, "What are you doing here?" "I wanted to bring you these flowers; I know a beautiful lady such as yourself deserves beautiful things!" Myra and Bernard ran to the window to see who their mother was talking to, Paula smiled and said. "You don't know me to be bringing flowers to my steps." "That's why I'm here to get to know you. Can you please come down so we could talk?" Myra said, "mom, is that the man from yesterday?" "Yes, now both of you get out of the window and mind your business!" Paula shouted to Homer, "Give me a minute and I'll be down." She told Myra to watch her brother. "Mommy that guy has flowers for you, can I have one please?" "Yes—I will be right back; don't let Bernard out of your sight." She took off her house slippers and put on some shoes and went down stairs, when he saw her at the front door he started to blush. He gave her the flowers and they sat on the front porch and talked; he was trying to persuade her to go on a date with him. That one day turned into six months of him trying for a date; everyone in the family got to know him. He was very generous and treated them like they were his own family, showering them with money and love. As time passed she began to gain trust in him. She liked his persistence. He was catching deep feelings for her and decided to come clean. He told her that he had been living with a woman; he tried to assure her that was all it was. She told him she didn't want any trouble and asked for him to leave. She wasn't putting up with being the second woman. She was very disappointed and hurt but all at the same time, she kept her head up in a womanly manner. He tried to assure her that he loves her and that no other woman ever made him feel like she did. What he didn't tell her, that he was a big time drug dealer and a part time pimp. Homer was a real slick talker and a charmer. However, when you play with other people feelings and emotions, karma will catch up with you. Homer didn't know how to feel now that his feelings were crushed. Homer had moved Paula into one of the apartment buildings that he owned, rent free and paid all of her extra bills. She didn't have to worry about paying for anything. Paula saved and banked all her money. After a year passed she realized that she was pregnant, she didn't let him know because she was having thoughts of aborting the baby, and she had no plans on bringing another child into this cold world. She went to the abortion clinic one day; while waiting her turn she got a message from God to give life to the child. Paula is a God fearing woman that didn't believe in abortions; at the time she thought it was best for her, being that she wasn't married to him, and he already having a live in woman. Paula sat there with tears slowly falling down her face, she thought to herself, "what am I doing here?"

She stood up and ran out of the clinic crying. As time passed she started to show. Homer was confused, he always thought he couldn't have any children; he was hurt, he thought the love of his life was pregnant by someone else. even after she told him the child was his, he didn't believe her, he asked. "Why didn't you tell me?" She tried to explain to him, he wasn't trying to believe her. Things became shaky and he stopped coming around and paying her bills. Paula was no fool though, she learned from past experience how men could be. When her brothers became aware of Homer's attitude they became upset because they knew their sister was a loyal woman. They told her about Homer being a drug dealer and pimp. They told her they keep it a secret because they knew she would've never taken advantage of a good situation. They didn't have any problem with Homer's hustles, they knew he wouldn't and couldn't turn Paula out. Beside they talked with him in the beginning and let him know that they knew about his hustle and that they would kill him if he ever tried anything with their sister. The Mills brothers where very well known as young and ruthless men. They were over protective over their sisters. The youngest Gene was buying drugs from Homer at half price. When she finished listening to her brothers filling her in about her baby's father she was shocked, she thought all his money was from his two apartment buildings. After this news, she wanted to get as far away from Homer as she could, so she decided to buy a house and continue to raise her family. She had enough money saved to afford a one family house on Littleton Avenue, it was perfect for her. She rubbed her stomach and promised herself that this would be her last child. She vowed to love her new child the same as her others, she gave birth to Lagant on December 5, 1969.

Inner Thoughts

Lagant drove home thinking about the amazing sex him and Star just had. He was smiling from ear to ear. He thought how can a female so gorgeous be single? He figured she probably has a boyfriend in Cali or somewhere, but he didn't let it bother him. He laughs; if she was your girlfriend she wasn't tonight, singing to himself. Tonight's escapade with Star made him feel like any women was gettable. He felt he was God's gift to women. He was ready to spread his wings and put his paw into any lady of his choosing. He wanted his cake and eat it too; he was ready to play the games that were made by women. He was changing. He was becoming a good guy going bad! His loyalty to women was gone. He could feel the Mack & Pimp blood flowing through his veins. Just that fast, he decided to turn from a loyal man to a player. As he drove through Virginia's fresh night air, it was as if a metamorphosis had just taken place.

When he arrived home, he went straight into the room. He took his clothes off and headed to the shower; he had a long day ahead of him. As the water ran down his firm muscular body, he started to think of the last few days; he was still puzzled as to why the doctor would congratulate him on having a boy. He flashed back to the look on Jada's face, she was definitely hiding something. He suppressed those thoughts and thought about his brother. He figured he'd call home tomorrow after he got Jada and the baby situated. As he was washing Star's sent off, the nurse popped in his head. "Oh—yeah! How could I forget about the nurse Parker? Shaped liked Serena Williams; I'd let her play with my balls and I'd like to play with her rack; he laugh to his self, thinking; nurse Parker could get It!"

He hoped to see Miss Parker tomorrow when he picks them up; he was ready to sow his royal oats and go for what he know. He knew he needed his own apartment soon; he was ready to put a harem in his stable, aim to be promiscuous.

Murder One

The whistle blew; the correction officers hit the panic button and radioed the center, calling in a code 33. They cleared the tier telling the inmates to lock in. When they approached cell #2015, there was a pool of blood in front, and Luis Rodriguez, aka Loco, laid stretched out with blood leaking out from his neck. The officer looked up and saw Anthony Smith, aka Rock, sitting on the bunk with a blade sticking out of his shoulder with blood running down. "Damn!—get help before I bleed to death this motherfucker tried to kill me!" "Help is on the way, try to stay calm!" Officer Carter tried to calm Rock down; he wanted to ask what happened but decided to wait until he received medical attention and then get a full statement from him. CO Carter had worked in the prison for 15 years, he could somewhat picture what went down. He knew Luis Rodriguez was out of place being in Anthony's cell; he was disappointed that it happened on his shift, now he had a lot of paper work to fill out.

The courts ended up charging Rock with murder and he lost his parole date. Khalil stood there in shock after Cool Breeze finished telling him the story. "Shit, better Loco died than Rock. We have to get him a lawyer, that's the only chance he has to see daylight. Damn! That's fucked up; my nigga was on his way home! I know it's a war about to break out in there?" "No the Amigos gave their word that there would be no retaliation. Loco was on his own when he made that hit, it wasn't a G call. Matter of fact, they gave Rock his props, they say Loco always finished his target." Cool Breeze looked at his Rolex and said, "Look blood, I love to sit here and politic with you more but I got to go and meet this chick. Keep your head up, and don't spend all your money on one bitch." They laughed and shook hands then hugged; Cool Breeze spent around and jogged to his red

Mustang convertible, jumped in and turned the radio up. Jay-z and Mary J's "Can't Knock the Hustle" was blaring thru the speakers. As he merked off he blew the horn twice and put his fist in the air. Khalil stood there thinking about Rock, "I have to get my dude a good ass lawyer."

Cotton Candy

At 8 o'clock the alarm clock rang, waking Lagant up from a comfortable sleep. He popped straight up; he was excited to be bringing his first born home, he went to freshen up. He put on a red & white Roc-a-Wear sweat suit with a new white tee shirt and his red on white high top Air Force Ones. He put on his red fitted cap and sprayed on some Obsession cologne, and was out the door. He first stop was McDonalds to order some breakfast for him and Jada. Miss Cotton the manager was working the drive thru window and handled his order quickly but not professionally, when he pulled up to the window she said, "Good morning your order is twelve dollars and fifty cents." He handed her a twenty dollar bill as he turned the radio down. "I love that song!" Lagant had R. Kelly's 12 Play pumping from the speakers; he read her named tag and responded. "You like this song, maybe I can give you some of my twelve play—Miss Cotton" with a devilish grin on his face. She smiled showing her deep indented dimples and pearly whites. He quickly grabbed his pen and wrote down his name and cell phone number while continuing to flirt with Miss Cotton. He had her blushing; he was very persuasive and persistent. She seemed to be in her early thirties with smooth dark skin and a shape like Buffy the Body, her ass looked as soft as her name. He took his change and the food then said, "Look if you find the time in your busy schedule, give me a call—I promise you it will be worth your time." She accepted the number and tried to pronounce his name but stumbled over it; he corrected her and said, "I hope to hear from you later dimples!"

When he arrived to the hospital Jada was feeding Iesha, she looked up and spoke. "Good morning daddy! Did you bring me breakfast baby?" "Yes, your favorite." "Thank you baby, I see you didn't forget the car seat."

"Of course not!" He sat in the chair next to Jada's bed and started eating his breakfast, "We're going to eat together baby girl," he said, talking to Iesha who was sucking her bottle like it was so good. An older nurse walked in, and Lagant thought about Miss Parker, he wanted to see her. The nurse asked, "How's the family? Are you ready to take your daughter home to meet her big brother?" Lagant paused and looked at Jada, Jada replied, "Yes I am!" He thought to himself where in the hell is this son that everybody knows about besides me? Jada's smile faded away fast and her eyes dropped down to Iesha. Jada spoke, "Mrs. Martin I'll ring the buzzer when we're ready." Lagant looked at Jada and started back eating his food; he want to ask about this son but decided to wait until she came clean. He wondered how long it was going to take her.

The Flashback

It was a normal morning at Shakur's house with his wife Pam getting the kids ready for school, while she prepared for work. Before leaving she told Shakur that she was going to pick up Junior after school, so call erica and tell her she doesn't have to pick him up today; Shakur's son spends every weekend with them. Shakur did his morning chores and got dressed in his work uniform and prepared himself for his morning drug transactions. He always handled all his deliveries in the morning, he like the mornings because people don't pay attention as much in the a.m. They are to focus on heading to their jobs. He puts his twin Smith & Wesson 45 automatics in his vest holder that he always wore under his uniform, and checks his order forms before starting his work day. Shakur would pull up to his customers in his P&P van and deliver buckets of paint according to their work order. It seemed to the watching eye that someone was just getting their house painted or paint delivered, when in reality its pure Columbian cocaine. After all orders were complete he would go to his hide out spot and put the money in his hiding safe. Then he stops at the P&P office to make sure things are running smoothly, and then off to Nubian Flavors, a small restaurant in the hood of Portsmouth that was famous for their halal food. Shakur knew the owner, Rashid and his younger brother Pop very well; they would sit and talk about everything under the sun, their conversation reminded you of a barbershop. He would leave in time to meet Starlette to open up at twelve o'clock.

Shakur needed someone that he could trust with his business so he sent for his only sister in California to help him. Both of his legal businesses pulled in good money, but he had become a millionaire mainly though his side hustles. He learned early in the game that there was jealousy, envy and hate that came from all directions, especially from the inner circle. He wasn't about to let anyone infiltrate his business. Coming up from the bottom he had to bury a lot of those types of people that was so-called down with him, to this day their bodies can't be found. He was smart and always ahead of his game, he was a thinker first, then a doer; and when he did it, he did it right!

Shakur had been in VA for nine years, he moved there from Cali with his baby's mother and their son Shakur Jr. His baby mother erica had family there; he moved to get away from his father who was openly cheating on their mother who allowed it. He figured it would be the best move for him before he did something to hurt his father. He got a construction job to support his family, and at work is the place he met the man that would change his life. Sam! Sam the owner of the construction company and also one of the biggest drug suppliers in Virginia, taught him all the in and outs of the business. Not the construction business, but the drug lord business. When Sam retired, he turned all of his connections over to Shakur and introduced him to all the necessary players in the game. Shakur always remembered the rules and sayings that Sam implanted in his head; with money comes power and with both comes great responsibility; the art of delusion, what the eyes see and the ears hear, the mind believes! Sam always told him when it's time for you to retire, you will be given a sign; don't ever take that sign lightly! Don't be greedy, pass the pie when its time, you will feel it in your heart and mind who to turn it over to, don't second guess yourself. Do as I do, teach the art to someone you can trust, and when you retire sit back and enjoy your wealth with your family.

Starlette pulled into the parking lot in her Lexus coupe, bopping her head and singing along with the music. As she was parking Shakur was opening up the gates to the Moonlight, as she approached him he asked. "What make you so happy this morning?" "I can't be happy Shakur?" "Of course you can sis its just I've never seen you this ecstatic before, especially about work." "I had a great night with my new friend last night, that's all." "So who's the lucky guy, anybody I know?" "I don't think so, his name is Lagant, and he's the perfect gentleman." "Where did you meet him at" "As a matter of fact I meet him in here." Starlette was smiling from ear to ear, while Shakur turned red. "What? Have you lost your mind, you fucking with one of the customers?!" "What's wrong with the customers? Their people too! And beside he's not really a customer it was his first time in here. He just stopped in after a hard day of work, Hell he still had on his navy uniform!" "You fucking with the biggest male whores there are! Don't you remember your father? How long have you known this guy? What can you tell me about him?" "Damn! One question at a time Shakur, you act like you don't want me to have a friend?" "No, sis that's not it I just don't want to bury one of them clown ass navy guys for trying to fuck you over!" "That's not going to happen—I'm grown and I can handle my own affairs of the heart, brother— You are so crazy!" Starlette took it as a joke but Shakur was dead serious. "Sis, I just don't want no man to hurt you in any way—I know how sweet and sensitive you can be—I don't want anybody to take advantage of you. I know I could be a little over protective, I'll try to work on that for you." "I understand—its okay." Shakur walked to the back to his office. Starlette started doing her daily routine. When she had a moment to herself, she thought about all the things her brother had said, she knew in many ways he was right, but then again, she knew she would follow her own heart. She wondered what Lagant was doing now?

The Home Coming

Lagant parked in front of their apartment complex with Jada and his new born daughter. Jada grabbed the baby bag and opened the door, while Lagant carried his little lady across the threshold. He started introducing her to the different rooms in their apartment, as if she could understand him. When he took her into her room he said, "Daddy has a surprise for you—How do you like your new crib?" As he placed soft kisses on her small cheeks he told her not to worry, daddy will teach you everything you need to know.

Jada went into their bedroom to get undressed for a shower, Lagant walked in showing Iesha their room. He looked up at Jada getting undressed and realized she had a new look to her, her womanly parts were bigger and rounder, he figured her new look was do to motherhood. He loved her body before but this extra weight made her look even sexier, he started to second guess his infidelity and breaking up with her. Once Jada started her shower Lagant continue talking to the baby. "Mommy is keeping a secret from us, but when I find out the truth about everything and you get old enough to handle the truth. I will let you know!"

Jada was enjoying her hot shower and wondering how she could begin to tell Lagant about her son. She wanted him to know everything from the beginning to the end; she needed to build up more confidence to go back down that painful road. Once she got older she was able to put her bad memories behind her: from her father leaving them; to meeting her double—crossing first love; along with her non—understanding mother. But the most depressing thing was being forced to give up on her own flesh and blood. Now she had to relive those painful memories all over again. She knew this was something that had to be done if she wanted to keep the love of her life and now new baby's father.

Itchy Feet

Paula called Alice's house looking for Bernard who wasn't there. She told Alice that Parole had just left her house, with the police, looking for him. Alice told her that she thought that he went to parole and she will have him call her when he gets back. (They hung up) Paula thought to herself, "What am I going to do with that boy? Why would he want to go back to prison? All he had to do was report to the parole office, that's it! Oh God! help me not to worry, and please protect my family."

Khalil was at a lawyer's office giving him all of Rock's information. The lawyer, Mr. Gills, told Khalil that he would look into it and handle everything, and that he had handled some cases just like this one and won. Khalil had heard about Mr. Gills while he was in prison and felt that he was the best lawyer for Rock's case. Mr. Gills charged him twenty thousand dollars to handle the case; Khalil gave him ten thousand up front and told him that he will get the rest after he wins the case. As Khalil was leaving the lawyers office his cell phone rung, it was Alice giving him the news about parole and the police looking for him. "Good looking baby—I was just about to head to my mother's house but not now!" "Why did you lie to me I thought you was reporting Khalil?" "Baby I didn't mean to lie to you, but I knew you wouldn't understand." "What are you going to do baby?" "Fuck parole they act like they my motherfuckin slave master. This ain't the slavery days! You just make the moves I told you about, I have a coupla stops to make and I'll be there!"

Khalil had Kunta Kinte in his blood and was ready to run from the pigs, his first stop was to Newark Penn Station. It was packed with all types of nationalities, it was loud and busy. Khalil waited at the back of the ticket line becoming very impatient. He spotted Penn Stations security, which was also Newark Police, walking through the crowd with their K-9's. He started to get nervous, he thought of the ounce of purple haze he had in his pocket. As they got closer, he started to think they were heading towards him. He was just about to turn around and walk out when he heard the female teller say "next in line." He looked at her and then again at the officers and was relieved when they turned down towards the tracks. After he purchased his tickets, he called his mother. "Mom, I talked to Alice she told me everything. Listen I don't want you to worry about me, I'm good!" Paula interrupted. "Boy! What's wrong with you; all you had to do was report to the man's office! All he wanted you to do was to get a job, and stay out of the streets! I don't understand you Bernard!" "Mom, I'm not worried—all they can do is send me back to finish the rest of my time. And that's nothing but a year and a half, but listen, I called to get Gant's number and to tell you that Alice is coming by to get my things." Paula gave him the information and said. "I love you Bernard don't do anything stupid and be safe!" Paula sat back after she hung up the phone. She knew exactly why he wanted Gant's phone number.

The Truth

Jada got out of the shower feeling refreshed, her thoughts were still a little cloudy but she knew it was time to tell Lagant the truth. As she entered the room Lagant was still singing and playing with Iesha, she watched his every move as she lotioned her body. "I feel so much better now." "You smell better too!" "Oh, you're trying to be funny Gant?" "No—not really; you smell better then what you did fifteen minutes ago." Lagant replied with a grin on his face, while Jada tossed a pillow at him. "You have jokes, huh? Let me see you give birth and come from the hospital smelling good!" "That's not going to happen; I make babies—not birth them! Call me a creator."

Jada prepared to feed Iesha while Lagant went into the living room and sat in his leather recliner. He brought it when they first moved in; he figured every man must have his own recliner if he was going to be king of his castle. He channel surfed until he found the Subway Series; the score was Yankees 10~~Mets 7. It was late into the ninth inning and Darrel Strawberry was up to bat. Lagant's eyes were glued to the game until Jada interrupted by grabbing the remote and turning the TV off just as Goose was pitching one of his curve balls. Lagant jumped up yelling, "turn it back on Jada! What the hell are you doing?" "Stop yelling before you wake the baby, I need to talk to you. It's important so can you please sit back down." "Damn!—this better be important!" "Yes it is."

He realized that Jada was finally coming clean with him about her son. He knew by ignoring her it would speed up the process. Jada sat on the love seat looking at him with the strangest look on her face; she didn't know where to start. All of her confidence that she was building up over the last few days was gone. Honestly, she didn't want to bring it back up again, and in a childish way she figured he didn't really want the truth because he never mentioned the situation to her.

"Jada are you alright?! You're sitting there looking stuck." "I'm wondering why you haven't given me a kiss, hug, or brought any flowers or balloons when I was in the hospital? I just gave birth to your daughter, and you've made me feel like I don't even exist! every other mother that was there had balloons and cards, besides me, that's the lease you could of done!"

Lagant sighed and looked at Jada like she was crazy; thinking to himself, this bitch has the nerve to try and switch it up on me, he knew she was trying to start an argument.

"enough Jada! I'm not beat for the bullshit— you know why!" She jumped up trying to hug him while crying and saying, I'm sorry—Can you please sit back down—I don't want to fight with you—it's about what the doctor said in the delivery room." Jada started telling Lagant the whole story making sure not to miss a single detail. Once she was finished, she apologized for not trusting herself enough to tell him earlier. "It still hurts me knowing that I have a son somewhere in this world; he will never know who I am and I will never know him." Lagant stood up and held her tighter than ever before.

Victoria's Dream Date

Victoria was outback stretching. She was wearing her black and white spandex exercise outfit. The morning was fresh; you could smell the red roses in the air. She and her best friend, Bones, were going on their weekly jog through a path in the woods that started in the back of her house and lead to the front. Victoria was thirty eight years old but looked only twenty five; if you were to see her and her daughter Susan you'd think they were sisters. As she jogged through the woods she started to plan her events for the day. She figured she would prepare herself brunch, then a nice hot shower, and then off to the mall. She wanted to buy a nice, sexy outfit for the date she was planning to arrange with Lagant.

She thought about when he told her to call anytime after five o'clock and she planned to do just that. The more she jogged, her thoughts became deeper. She thought how she had never been with a black man (sexually) before, but had always desired and wondered what it would be like. Victoria wasn't prejudiced. However, growing up in her society, being with a black man was not permitted. But now, being a grown woman, divorced, single and free, she had realized that variety is the spice of life. The day she saw Lagant at the hospital she knew he was the one to add that spice to her life. She thought about his baby's mother and had come to the conclusion that she was willing to share him if she had to. It was time for her to get what she wanted and she was ready to play the game.

As she finished her jog, she always did one walk around her 15,000sq ft house to catch her breath. She lived in an extravagant, private community. The house, along with alimony and child support, was part of her divorce settlement. Victoria's bank account reached seven digits; she kept her job because she loves what she does and was content with her lifestyle. The

71

only thing that was missing was a man; she was planning on filling that void very soon. At the mall she picked out a red silk spaghetti strap shirt that revealed her cleavage and a pair of Bailey stretch jeans that hugged her body. The sales clerk helped her pick out the perfect pair of red stilettos that strapped around the ankle, then a red, white and blue silk scarf that she will wear as a belt. As she was exiting the mall she couldn't resist the new Louis Vuitton bag; she knew it would add the touch she needed to her sexy outfit. Victoria was ready for Lagant. Her confidence, beauty and her winning attitude were all in check.

The Test

Lagant continued to hug Jada as the tears poured down her face. Just the same as the day that she had to give her son up for adoption. All she could say was, "I'm sorry!" over, and over again. It was like she was apologizing to her son and Lagant all at the same time, through her cries. "everything will be okay Jada, you have to pray about it, ask God to strengthen you in your weakness-you must understand it wasn't your fault—You were young—it was nothing you could have done! I know it must have been difficult for you." Lagant had sympathy for Jada and he tried to comfort her as best he could. "Do you forgive me Gant?" "Yes, I forgive you! The question is do you forgive yourself?" She paused and thought to herself, "NO! It could have been different, now I'll never know my own flesh and blood." She started back crying uncontrollably while holding Lagant for dear life.

"Jada! You have to get a hold of yourself! Is there any way you can find him?" "I don't think so. It's been so long ago and even if I do, what will I say to him?" "Jada I can't answer that but if it hurts you so, I know you will find the right words to say!" "I don't even know how to go about it. Where would I start Gant?" "Jada if there's a will, there's a way!"

Jada slowly began to regain her composure. She was still crying and watching Lagant's every move, trying to read his body language. Lagant was sitting in his recliner looking like a physiologist to Jada. She was wondering what was on his mind.

"Gant do you still love me?" Jada mumbled. "Why would you ask me a question like that? I must admit-I'm very disappointed in you—you kept something that important away from me for so long and you lied to me! Worst of all, I had to find out from the doctor that you had a son! My question to you is: do you have any other secrets or any other lies that you need to tell me about? especially after I've shared my deepest and darkest secrets with you!" "Yes—I know!" "evidently, you don't!—look, you still lying to me! Are you going to tell Iesha about her brother when she's older?"

Jada had never thought that far ahead about the situation; she couldn't answer his question. She grabbed the sofa pillow and balled up in the middle of the couch. Lagant looked at Jada and thought to himself, "I wonder what else this girl is capable of?" He went into the bedroom and laid in the bed and started to reminisce about all the negative things Jada had put him through. He thought about the time she tested his loyalty by having one of her girlfriends push up on him at the club. Jada set him up good, or so she thought.

He flashed back to the night when he and Tino and their Navy crew from Newark were having a guy's night out at a club named Picasso. Jada called on her friend Maria; a drop dead gorgeous Latina chick whom they called a pint sized Jennifer Lopez. She showed Maria a picture of Lagant and gave her all the information that she thought she would need to bait him. Maria had on her sexiest outfit, fish net stockings and a one piece Baby Phat black mini dress that hug her curve with some black stilettos that strapped her calves. Her hair was styled in a Chinese bun with two long hair pins that favored chop sticks through the bun. She was sexy and seductive, looking very provocative and had a confidence that her target would bite.

When Maria arrived at the club the bouncer saw her walking towards the back of the line and called her out. "Ma-Ma, come here, a lady like you don't stand in line here at Picasso. You receive VIP status here, take this pass and show it to the cashier at the window; she'll point you to the VIP section." Once she got in the club the music started to vibrate through her body. As she walked guys were trying to talk to her left and right but she didn't pay them any attention. She was on the hunt for her target. It took her fifteen minutes to spot him in the corner by the bar with his crew.

Lagant was watching all his boy's get turned down by the finest looking Latina woman in the club. He was laughing to himself and calling them fools. He knew he wasn't going to ask her for a dance after he'd seen his whole crew get kicked to the curb. He figured he was good just by admiring her sight of beauty from afar. Maria finally made it through the pack of wolves and stopped in front of Lagant by the dance floor. The dance floor was packed with party goers dancing to "It's time for the Percolator." He was checking her out from head to toe, when she started to move her body from side to side like a snake. He was enjoying the view and the scent of strawberry that lingered from her as she moved to the music. One of his friends told him to ask her to dance, but he was afraid of being shot down. He looked at his drink and yelled to his crew, "I'll be back I'm heading to the bar!" Maria overheard him and said, "That sounds like a good idea, Papi." Looking him directly in his eyes letting him know that she was talking to him. Lagant was confused; he looked over his shoulders to see if she was talking to him or someone else. He point to his self "Who me?" Maria winked her eye and perked out her lips and nodded her head yes. "Sure gorgeous what can I get you?" "I'll have whatever your drinking, Papi!"

She walked over to him placed her hands on his chest and asked his name. He replied with his nick name from back home everyone called him when growing up, "Babyface." He used his nick name when he was out partying. Maria was confused; because Jada told her his name was Lagant. She looked at his face again to make sure she had the right person. She knew it was him; he matched her photographic memory of the picture Jada had given her. She figured he was using an alias. "I like your name and your silk shirt. My name is Maria but you can call me Kat that's my nickname." She was rubbing her hands up and down his shirt, and then she waved her hand for him to give her his ear, she purred in his ear like a cat and finished it off with a meow, while scratching down his back. Maria was flirting, giving him her best performance and Lagant was eating it up.

"Papi—who you come here with?" "I came with my friends, but right now I'm with you!" "I like that Papi, but are those thugs your friends?" "Yeah, they good guys." She looked at him and said, "I came by myself, I need a friend to party with, will you be my friend?" "Yeah, Kat—I'll be your friend!" The bartender interrupts and asks, "What can I get you?" Two "Long Island Ice Teas." "So, Kato do you have a girl?" "Yes I do." "If you won't tell-I won't tell— what she doesn't know can't hurt her— right." "Your right about that, but I vowed to myself to try to be loyal." "I understand Papi—but promises are made to be broken! You don't like what you see?" She turned around and did a 360 in slow motion, spinning with her hands on her hips. "You would let all of this pass you by Kato?" Maria placed her hands on his shoulders and gave him a big thank you kiss for her drink. "I have a VIP pass, would you like to be my guest so we can sit down and become more acquainted, Papi?" He loved her accent and how she kept calling him Papi. "Sure Kat, we are important people, lead the way!"

She held his hand and led him to a private, cozy section of the VIP lounge. There were plush leather love seats and drapes that sectioned off the area for privacy. She sipped on her drink, it was her first time having a "Long Island Ice Tea", and it tasted sweet to her. She was drinking it like it was only sweet iced tea. She didn't have any idea it was made with seven different liquors. They sat on the love seat as she was performing her best seduction acts ever on him. She had him open. They were dancing; she was backing it up on him making his nature rise. She was feeling herself! By her third "Long Island Ice Tea", she was toasted! She wiped the sweat from his forehead and looked him in the eyes. "Papi, you're so fine!" She moved in closer and started kissing him; with the mixture of his charm and the drinks all combined, she honestly forgot why she was there.

Maria took his hand and placed it in between her thighs, helping him to locate her steaming center, while she stroked his manhood. She was drunk and horny without realizing it. She had his solider at attention, "Owww Papi, I like it hard like this!" Then she unzipped his zipper and pulled out his manhood and sat on his lap. As she eased down onto the donkey, Lagant helped her with every move to ensure a perfect delivery; she rode him like a rodeo cowgirl. They didn't care about fucking in the club; no one was paying them any attention. even if they were, it looked as if Maria was giving him a real intense lap dance. Maria was enjoying the excitement fucking in the club so much she began to orgasm back to back. every time she felt it coming down, she would lean forward putting her hands on the coffee table, look over her shoulder and moan, "Papi— Fuck this pussy cat!"

Lagant loved the way she sounded and moved her pelvic muscle while talking in Spanish to him. He felt his soldier ready to burst; Maria was talking in tongues. She leaned back and put her arm around his head and blurted out, "this is why Jada' stuck on you Lagant!" She wasn't thinking, she tried to cover it up. She started speaking back in Spanish to try to throw him off. After he released his bomb inside of her, he gripped her by the neck to stop her from moving. He wanted to comment on her statement, but it was feeling so good to him, he erupted again, he reached over with one arm and wrapped it around her waist, with his arm around her neck leaning her back. He had heard every word that just came from her mouth. "What the fuck did you just say? How do you know Jada, and how in the hell do you know my name? Oh!—bitch you trying to set me up?" "Sorry Papi, I'm so sorry, I can explain!"

Maria sat on the coffee table facing Lagant and told him not to get upset; that she was going to keep it real with him. She spilled the beans on how Jada sent her to test his loyalty, Lagant was furious with Jada. He told Maria that it wasn't her fault, Maria promised not to tell Jada what had happened between them. "I'm not trying to make any excuses, but the drink and your charm. I became excited and extra horny, I had to have you. Please don't tell Jada!" "Don't worry; I'm not going to mention a word to Jada. This is one test I don't mind failing, just tell Jada that I passed." Maria told Lagant she had to leave; on the inside she was feeling sluttish. When she reached the steps to exit the VIP lounge, she looked back and thought. "Who was the target, him or me?"

Lagant on the other hand, didn't feel bad, he had told her that, "he vowed to TRY and be loyal." But everyone knows a man is going to be a man, especially when the cat falls right into his lap. The sad part is the pussy cat was sent by his own girl. Lagant sat on the leather love seat smiling, "Thank you Jada for the gift and it's not even my birthday." The next day when Jada asked Maria about how Lagant reacted, with a straight face she replied; "All I could get out of him was a couple of dances, he seemed drunk and he was mainly partying with his boys." Lagant fell asleep thinking of the test of loyalty then wondered could he ever be loyal again.

Shakur Meets Sis New Friend

The phone rang in Lagant and Jada's apartment; Jada answered on the first ring. "Hello." "What's up Jada, how are you doing? Congratulations, how does it feel being a mother?" "It feels good, but who is this?" "It's Khalil." "Oh! Hey Khalil, it's been a while since I've talked to you, how does it feel being home?" "It feel good, I'm free like a bird, no more locked doors!" They both laughed, "Sis, where my brother?" "He's in the room asleep." "Okay, don't wake him just let him know that I'm coming down tomorrow. I'll call from the train station to tell him what time I will arrive. Is it alright with you?" "Sure Khalil, you know you're always welcomed here!" "I need to see my little niece, Iesha!" "That's nice your coming to see her, I'll let Gant know as soon as he wakes up." "Okay sis, I'll see y'all tomorrow." "Ok Khalil, tell the family I said hi!"

Jada hung up and went into the kitchen to make lunch for her and Lagant. It was almost time to wake Iesha for her evening feeding. Lagant was awakened by the vibration of his cell phone. He looked at his phone, he had two missed calls. They were both from Starlette. Lagant checked his messages: "I'm missing you baby, I enjoyed our time together last night, I was just thinking about you. I'm at work now, so call me when you get a chance, ok sweetie." Lagant thought to himself, "Let the games begin."

Lagant was ready to scratch and sniff what the world had to offer. He erased the messages, just in case Jada got on some sneaky shit. He got up and went to freshen up, then walked into the living room and saw Jada, red eyed and feeding Iesha. "I made you a turkey sandwich, it's in the refrigerator." "Good looking Jada, I could use a bite to eat." He bent over and gave his daughter a kiss, then proceeded to the kitchen for his lunch. "I told you we going to eat together baby girl." When he finished eating he grabbed his Roca Wear sweat suit jacket and red fitted cap. "Where are you going?" "I promised Tino that I would help him set up his web site today." "Do you know how long you'll be gone?" "It shouldn't be long." He bent down and gave Iesha a kiss on her forehead. "Daddy will be home later, take care of you mother." "I don't get a kiss?" Lagant bent back down to kiss Jada on her forehead, but she lifted her head so her lips could meet his. His eyes became wide; Jada didn't know how to feel. "I love you, be safe." "Ok." He walked out the door, Jada couldn't read his body language like she use to, but she did sensed a change in him.

Lagant was headed to the Moonlight, to surprise Star; he pulled into the parking lot and was fortunate to get a space across from Starlette's Lexus. He walked in and felt a little awkward in his sweat suit; it was a nice, mature and sophisticated crowd. "Fuck it; I'll be the rock star this evening!" He sat at the bar and watched almost every guy at the bar push up on Star. He knew it was about to be a lot of upset motherfuckers once she noticed he was there. Almost every guy she waited on tried to flirt with her. They were on her like bee's on honey, but Star kept a beautiful smile on her face as she listened to them flirt.

She was so pre-occupied with blocking out the unwanted chatter, when she got to Lagant, she looked up to ask what he wanted to drink and jumped like she'd seen a ghost. He was the last person she was expecting to see. She was so excited, she reached over and hugged and kissed him. All the men at the bar were shocked to see her react like she just did with some unknown man. They looked like—who the hell is that? She gave Lagant a Corona and two shots of Henny. She had lots of questions for him but couldn't get them out like she wanted to, with the customers ordering drink after drink. "Am I going to see you tonight when I get off?" "Star, I want to bad as hell. But you know I brought my daughter home today, and I at least want to put her to sleep on her first night home." "I know, I know, sorry baby, I'm not trying to be selfish." "Boo, it get's greater later, believe me!" Star rubbed his hand, "Your right baby."

Shakur was looking at the way his sister was interacting with Lagant; he was feeling uneasy as he watched all the attention she was giving him. He figured that had to be the guy Star was talking about. Shakur walked over to the bar, "what's going on? You have other customers waiting to be served! I'll take care of him; you go and handle the others." She looked at Shakur like he was crazy, but he wasn't paying her any mind, he was focused on Lagant. All Shakur could think about was what she saw in this dude? Who was this wanna be rap star that's supposed to be in the navy? He figured it had to be through a court order, {"He looks like one of them knuckle head gang bangers from New York."} He stood there cleaning a glass, "How you doing this evening, sir? Let me know when you need something else to drink. Wait let me guess, you want something sweet like a—sex on the beach-" Lagant clinched his teeth and gave Shakur a hard stare while thinking to himself; {"This sarcastic ass, player hating, motherfucker! He must want to feel my blade go across his face! On the strength of Star working here, I'm not going to bring any trouble to her job; I don't want her getting fired because of me."} Lagant replied sarcastically, "I'll wait to have that sex on the beach with my Boo, Star!"

Shakur became furious; he reached over the bar and grabbed Lagant by his jacket, pulling him halfway over the bar. Before Shakur could say a word, he felt a sharp object sticking him under his chin. "Let me the fuck go, or kiss your tongue goodbye!" Shakur's anger was quickly immobilized, he released Lagant's jacket and put his hands in the air showing that he'd surrendered. Lagant stood up with the five inch switch blade still held under Shakur's chin and said. "I don't want any trouble, but I'll take a double shot of Henny & Coke with three ice cubes—Thank you!" He quickly pocketed the blade, just as fast as he had pulled it out. It disappeared in a blink of an eye; a few drops of blood dripped form Shakur's chin. The guy sitting next to Lagant stared in amazement.

It happened so fast only a couple of people witnessed it. Starlette even missed it; she was in the back getting another bottle of Remy Martin. When she returned she could tell that something was wrong. Lagant was now standing, looking her brother directly in the eyes. And Shakur was holding a towel underneath his chin. "Is everything okay?" "Yeah, I just scratched a bump under my chin that's all." "everything's good baby, me and Shakur was just getting a little acquainted with each other." Lagant read his name tag from his P&P work uniform. "Take his order Star; I'm going in the back to clean this scratch."

As he walked to the back, Lagant was on point. He thought to himself, "I hope he don't try to do nothing stupid." "Yea baby, give me a double shot of Henny & Coke. This my last drink before I roll out." "You're leaving already!?" "Yeah—I just stopped by to surprise you—I wanted to see my shining 'star' today." "Ohhh, that's so sweet." Starlette turned to make his drink, Lagant started to think maybe Shakur was one of Star's ex's the way he reacted. She brought his drink in a big glass, "This one's for Iesha, so drive safe and if you can't drive, I'm calling you a cab!" "Nah if I can't drive you taking me home with you!" She reached for his drink, "Oh, if that's the case let me put some more liquor in it!" "You are trying to give me alcohol poison!" "No—but I am trying to get you to come home with me." "Don't tempt me Star." "I'm just playing—go home to your little star."

Shakur went into his office, reached inside his desk and grabbed one of his twin Smith & Wesson 45 automatics. He took the safety off and put one bullet into the head and tucked it into his waist. He walked back to the bar and saw Starlette smiling and talking to Lagant. He was upset that Lagant had gotten one up on him. Shakur planned on following Lagant after he left the club and putting one in him. Shakur thought about his actions, he started to realize that his sister was happy with this guy. He was staring, trying to figure out what Lagant motive was. He didn't want his little sister to get hurt, nor fall victim to a love scam. Shakur was just interested in him because of his sister. Lagant could feel Shakur watching their every move, but Lagant didn't pay too much attention to him just enough to stay on point. Lagant just added him to the list with all the rest of the muthafuckas who was envious of the attention he was receiving from the pretties' barmaid there; which made him feel special in a crazy way. He jokingly said. "I don't know Star—I don't think I can drive. It looks like you have to take me home with you." "Keep playing and you won't be kissing your daughter in the morning!" Lagant reached over and gave her a wet tongue kiss, ending it with three small wet kisses. "I hate to leave." She hit him with one of his saying, "Baby, it get's greater later, (They smiled at each other) call me around nine thirty and drive safe." "You got it baby; I'll talk to you then." He turned and walked toward the door and felt Shakur staring harder than Starlette was. His phone started vibrating, he looked at the phone number, and he couldn't identify it. "Hello." He opened the door leaving the Moonlight, letting the door swing close behind him.

Parkers Plot

Victoria returned from the mall with her new outfit in hand. She was ready to convert into the eye candy that she really was. After her shower, she took her time getting dressed she picked out her matching red laced thong & bra set. She loved how the red complimented her skin tone. Once she put on her stockings, she sat down and carefully chose the right shades of make-up to give her the more sensual sex appeal that she desired. She looked in her full length mirror; she liked her transformation and loved how her red stilettos elongated her legs. She sprayed her favorite perfume, White Diamonds, and then stepped into it. She topped her look off with some of her expensive jewelry. She was ready for what she knew was going to be a date, she wasn't taking no for an answer. She reached into a small paper bag and pulled out a 12 pack of condoms and smiled to herself then said, "It's on!" She was set; all she had to do was make the call. She reached in her work bag to retrieve his number but couldn't find it. She back tracked her thoughts and figured she left the pad at work; she rushed off to the hospital.

When she got off the elevator all eyes were glued to her, the doctors and nurses couldn't believe their eyes. Was this the same Miss Parker that they work with? They all spoke and she returned the hellos. One of the male nurses was coming out of a patient's room, and was caught off guard. "What's up Miss Diva?" "What did you call me?" "You look like a diva, girl! Who's the lucky man?" "What makes you think there's a man?" "For one, I know your straight, you like what I like." "Stevie you know that's a sin." Stevie gave her a stiff look and rolled his eyes. "We all sin, maybe in different ways, but sin is sin! So tell me who's the lucky man? Is it someone I'd date? You know how I like mines; tall dark and handsome!" Victoria laughed; Stevie always humored her with his gayness. "Stick to your man!" "Two is better than one Hun and the way you're dressed, I know he's fine. You don't mind sharing him do you? The three of us could have lots of fun!" She stopped walking and gave Stevie a beaming stare. "You know I'm just messing with you. Where's he taking you? May I ask?" "Mind your business. Who said I was going on a date?" "The way you look and smell, with those five inch heels on! If they don't say come and get me—I don't know what does!"

Victoria was smiling as she checked the nurse's station looking for the pad, she was on a mission. "I'm not trying to pry, but what are you looking for?" "If you must know I left something that I need. Ok?" "You don't have to tell me twice, I get the hint." Stevie walked off trying to switch his 140lb, Philippine body. She checked her office, even the garbage. She double checked and found the pad inside of a patient's folder but no phone number. She couldn't remember where she placed the number, she sat down and sighed. She thought to check Jada's file. She found everything but his cell phone number; she sat wondering what to do next.

She decided to have Stevie make the call; she paged him to her office. "What can I do for you Miss Parker?" "Take a seat." "Oh goodie, I get to play patient today!" She explained the whole situation to him and pleaded with him not to tell a soul! "I promise—I put it on girl power—I won't tell a soul!" "You're not a girl!" "I don't have to have a split to be a chick." "Whatever!—you just remember lose lips make fat lips." "Oh-no! — You don't have to worry about me—this is me and you're secret—You don't do anything but work, it's time for you to have some fun. I've seen the guy you're talking about, you sure you don't need any help?" "Shut up Stevie! My man doesn't interact like that!" "Look at you, already claiming him! You go—girl." "Stevie!" "I'm just teasing Miss Parker. Give me that phone. I'm about to get professional."

Cotton Plays Chest

"Hello, is this Mr. 12 play?" A soft soprano voice spoke clearly over the cell phone; he remembered the twelve play conversation with Miss Cotton, the manger of McDonalds. He was surprised to hear from her, she sounded sexy as hell over the phone. Lagant looked behind as he walked to his car; he was still being on point with Shakur. "I have more than 12, but if that's all you asking for then just maybe I could be of assistant!" "Oh really!" He smirked, and then said. "Yes really! "Um" "How are you doing Miss Cotton?" "Oh, you remembered" "Yes, why wouldn't I. I'm surprised your pretty self called, I was hoping that you would." "Well—you were able to put a smile on my face usually no one can do that especially in the mornings, then to top it off you had my husband playing from your car—I see you have good taste in music." "Your husband! You don't even know R Kelly—You meant to say, you seen your future husband driving the car!" "Future husband, how could you say that—I don't know you, Le-get!" She stuttered trying to pronounce his name. He tried to help her with it and she still couldn't say it correctly. Lagant suggested that he could come over and help her pronounce it correctly. "Are you trying to come over my house?" "That is only if I am invited."

Lagant was still sitting in the parking lot of the Moonlight Club, he felt comfortable sitting in his car flirting on the phone as he watched the beautiful ladies walk into the club. "Tell me, why I should invite a stranger into my home." "How else would you get to know your future husband?" "No! You can't answer a question with a question, I need an answer!" "Ok, you right. First off; it's still early in the day—Secondly; I'm not really a stranger, we did meet earlier and you could see with your own eyes—I'm not any murderer or rapist or no psychopath—Besides, you would be able to read my body language better in person instead of trying to figure me out over the phone." He paused to let what he just told her sink in, and then he said. "Besides, I'm bored—I would like to talk to you face to face— It doesn't have to be at your house, we could meet anywhere." She asked. "Where are you from?" "I'm from Jersey." "I have family in Newark." "You do, where at?—I'm from the Bricks"{Bricks is the nickname for Newark} "I figured you weren't from Virginia by the way you talk—The guys here talk with a southern accent— So what brings you to VA?" "The Navy." "Oh, no! I can't have any dealings with anyone in the navy—they go out to sea too much for me." "Don't worry Miss Cotton, I'm about to get out very soon, besides, I'm on shore duty. The ship days are over—so I'll be right here on dry land with you, baby!" "I heard about you navy guys—ya'll some . . . I'm not going to say it, I know you hear it enough." "What whores; that's an old rumor that is always going to stick—Me personally—I think they are a bunch of gay dudes." "How could you say that, and your in the Navy?" "I'm not talking about me! Not even everybody, but I call them gay cause its so many people sucking up and brown nosing so much that it just disgusts me!"

She listened as he talked, trying to get a feel of him through their phone conversation. She was a good judge of character and so far she liked everything that she was hearing. She admired the confidence he had in his voice. "Do you have a girlfriend?" "No— but I'm not going to lie, Miss Cotton." She interrupted him, "You could call me by my first name, and it's erica." "Ok, Miss erica Cotton, I like your last name, it fits you so well." "Why?" "Because your body looks soft, just like name." "I don't know if I should thank you or what?" "No!—Don't thank me—thank your mother! She's the one that blessed you with it." She smirked and then said, "Okay, getting back to my original question." "Oh-okay, I have a situation—My baby's mother and I still live together—I didn't get my own place, yet." "Oh—really!" She said with a curious voice. "Is that a problem for you erica?" "Yes, that's a major problem!—So, when you planning on getting your own place?" "A.S.A.P!-I got to find a spot first." "How old are you *Laget*?" "I see you still need help saying my name—I'm 22; am I too old for you?" She couldn't help but to laughing, "I'm sorry I keep mispronouncing your name—it's just that I've never heard a name like yours before— but I got you by nine years—now how are you too old for me? You're a young buck, do you think you could handle a grown woman such as myself?" "Just say I'm blessed! But I like older women because of the wisdom they have to offer and their sexual expertise. (He wanted to add their financially independent; he kept that to himself) Remember now—R Kelly only has 12 plays, I have more—so yes, I can handle a woman of your stature." "Well we will have to wait and see." "I have patience."

They were both enjoying each others conversation; it was going on thirty minutes of talking and flirting. It was dust dark as he looked around the parking lot he noticed two guys moving strangely around Starlette's Lexus. Lagant notice they were trying to break into her car. They didn't notice Lagant sitting in his car when they pulled out the jimmy and tried to break into her Lexus. He hit the button to his stash box and retrieved his 380 automatic and took it off safety. "I'll call you right back erica, I have to handle something real quick." Lagant quickly opened his car door and crept over to Star's car. The thief was bent over trying to jimmy the door. His back was turned to Lagant. He didn't hear or see him coming until it was too late; the lookout guy didn't notice either. When he did see Lagant, he pulled his glock nine and pointed it at Lagant telling him to back up. His partner looked up then stood straight up, right into Lagant's choke hold. Lagant put the gun to the guy's temple, "Don't move, or I'll blow your fucking brains out!" "Let him go or I'll shoot your ass." "We can handle these two ways; you can drop your gun and walk off and I'll let him go, or we can make it bloody!—Your choice." "No, let him go!" Lagant whispered in the guy's ear, "Your friend doesn't want you to live." The guy yelled to his partner, "Put the gun down! put the motherfucking gun down!"

The guy hesitated; he slowly put the gun down and stood with his hands in the air. "Put your hands down and kick the gun towards me." He did just as Lagant said then yelled, "Now, let him go!" "Go ahead start walking, this Lexus is off limits. If anybody fucks with it I'm coming for your head." Lagant then took the gun and hit the guy in back of the head with the handle. The blow knocked the guy to his knees. "Damn! You weak in the knees ass nigga, I thought this shit only happened in the movies." Lagant quickly picked up their Glock 9, jumped into his car and pulled out of the parking lot smoothly. As he drove off he called Starlette to inform her of what had just happened, but it went to voicemail. She called right back, "What's up baby?" "Yeah boo, go check on your car, two guys just tried to steal it. I bust one of guy's in the back of his head." "Oh my God, you shot him!" "No, it didn't get that far, I just hit'em. I don't know what they will try to do next, so take someone with you to check on it. Call me back and let me knows everything is ok."

Professional Call

The phone was ringing off the hook at Lagant and Jada's apartment. "Hello" "Hello, this is Steven Crow from Portsmouth Naval Hospital, may I speak to Miss Jada Willis please?" "This is she." "Ok, Miss Willis our records show that you just gave birth on the 24th of this month. I'm calling to complete some information we need for our records. I see we have all of your info, being the mother. But may I ask is the father known?" "Yes, he is." "Ok, we need his whole name and contact numbers." Jada gave him all the information, including his job and cell phone number as emergency contacts. "Does he live at the same address or does he reside elsewhere?" "No, same address." "Ok, thank you Ms. Willis. Sorry for disturbing you so late. Do you have any questions?" "No." "Ok, that will be it and congratulations on your daughter." "Thank you."

Stevie had put on one of his best performances; he gave Victoria the information then bragged, "Girl, I got more than his cell phone number!—and if you didn't know, you better watch yourself because he lives with her—well they live together—You know us girls have to stick together." "Stevie you're a doll, and remember keep this between us!" "My pink lips are sealed—just remember me when I need a favor!" "I will and thanks again, I'll see you on Monday!" She quickly exited the hospital, while Stevie thought to himself. "I knew Miss Parker was a freak under that uniform."

Victoria sat in her BMW and kissed the paper with Lagant's info on it. And then she lifted up the arm rest to place the number inside. There she discovered his original number and felt so stupid. She sat and gathered her thoughts; she didn't want anything else to go wrong tonight. She decided to go to T.G.I.F to get something to eat and a few cocktails to help build up her confidence before she called Lagant. Besides, it was only seven o'clock.

Fore Play

erica waited by the phone hoping that Lagant would call back, twenty minutes had already passed. She was becoming impatient; she didn't like how their conversation had ended. She felt that she had waited long enough, so she called him back. Lagant was driving with no destination in sight when his phone rang; he thought it was Star calling back. He looked at the phone and saw it was erica. With all the excitement he had forgot to call her back. "What's up Miss Cotton, I was just about to call you back, but you beat me to the punch. I bet you fast with your hands too?" "I don't play with my hands—What took you so long to call back? If you didn't want to come over . . . ." "Hold—hold—hold up!—who said that I didn't want to come over! Calm down, you know I want to see you! I just had to handle something—that's all." "Are you alright? You didn't get yourself into any trouble, did you?" "No, everything is good—now let me have your address." She gave him her address; he knew how to get there. She lived in the suburbs of Portsmouth. "I'm thirty minutes away, have your porch lights on." "Ok, just drive safe." "I got the wheel like a NASCAR driver—feel me?" erica jokingly said, "How could I feel you, and we're on the phone?" "Oh, I'll be there a.s.a.p, and then you could feel all over me." "That's not going on over here, were just going to talk—so don't get no crazy ideas, no touchy feely shit!" "My bad, I thought you wanted to feel me." "Just get here, and don't be long—I'll be waiting."

Lagant hung up the phone and imagined rubbing erica all over her body; he stopped at the gas station to full up his tank. He figured with his luck anything could jump off, so he picked up a box of Magnum condoms just in case. In the mean time, erica was tidying up the house; she sprayed some strawberry air freshener to finish it off. She couldn't believe she invited him to her house so soon, but their phone conversation made her feel so comfortable with him. It was like they already knew each other. In the back of her mind she really wanted to know more about his 12 play, but only if he played his cards right.

He arrived at erica's house and parked under a tall oak tree just pass her house. He turned off the car when his phone started to vibrate. And to his surprise it was Jada. "What's up Jada is everything ok?" "Yes, Iesha and I are just bored; we want our daddy—When are you coming home?" "I'm almost finished with Tino's computer—but listen—he wants to take me out and celebrate the birth of my first born—I accepted his invite, so kiss my daughter for me and don't wait up. Get some rest I'll be home later." "Oh, Gant, before I forget; your brother called and he will be here tomorrow, he's going to call from the train station for you to pick him up." "Ok—he didn't give you a time?" "No, he said that he'll call when he gets here." "Alright" "have fun and tell Tino I said hello—I love you." "Ok Jada."

Lagant ended the call just like that. Jada place the phone down figuring he was still upset with her and just needed a little time to blow off some steam. She didn't have any idea of the way he was blowing off his steam. Lagant decided to call Star back so there wouldn't be any interruptions between him and erica. "Hi baby, I'm sorry I didn't call you back, when my brother and I got outside to my car, all of my car windows were busted—My brother caught them and beat the crap out of them, I had to stop him. It was blood on my car; they stumbled away holding each other up. I felt sorry for them. I called the police to make a complaint; I need it for the insurance. So now I'm waiting on the tow truck—I'm sorry baby, it's just so much going on right now—I didn't even ask if you were ok." "Yeah—I'm good. My main concern is you—Are you ok?" "Yes baby—thanks to you they didn't steal my car!" "When I left your windows weren't busted out. Why did you call your brother down there when you had all your fans at the bar?" "My brother was here—the one that had on the green P&P work uniform." "Oh—that's your brother?" "Yes boo." Lagant thought; that's why he was acting like that. He was glad that he hadn't stabbed him; Star would have never forgiven him for that. "Why didn't you tell me?" "I don't know-(She wanted to keep them far apart from each other, knowing how her brother feels about any man) I was excited to see you—it just slipped my mind, I do have one question—How did you know they were trying to steal my car? You left over thirty minutes before you called me." Lagant had to think quickly. "Oh, I ran into one of my dudes when he was on his way inside. We were catching up and when I was about to leave I saw the two guys looking at your car, funny." "Well I'm happy you were there and that you're ok— I'm working until closing tonight—my brother is taking me home, so I'll call you tomorrow, okay baby." She blew a kiss threw the phone. "Ok baby, but if you need me for anything call me." "Okay I will-bye babe."

Lagant thought to himself—perfect, Star's good, Jada's good— now let the games begin! Now lets me make sure erica's good. He placed his phone on silent; he didn't want it to blow his chances with erica. He rung the bell, and was mesmerized by her body. He could tell from her work uniform that she had a nice body but it was more than he'd imagined. "What's wrong?" erica said, "Nothings wrong, I was just wondering where you been all my life?" She smiled and invited him in; he looked around her front room and said, "You have a beautiful home." It was nice and clean and smelled good. She had a lot of expensive furniture and he noticed a picture on the mantel of a young boy with a white and green baseball uniform on and asked, "Is that you little man?" "Yes, that's my son, Junior, he's ten years old. He stays with his father on the weekends." "That's good that his father is in his life" He continued looking around at all of the different African sculptures, her home was very afro-centric. He returns his attention back to erica. "Wow—look at you! You look like corned beef with macaroni & cheese and collard greens on the side!—My Nubian Queen!" She smiled and said, "You must be hungry!" "No-but you look finger licking good" Lagant said, while licking his lips. erica thought to herself, "Keep talking slick and I'll have you tasting my kitty."

erica was dressed in an "aeropostale" white halter top, black spandex bottoms with a pair of leather open toe sandals. Her toes were neatly pedicured and she had a French manicure, her top showed just enough cleavage. She was simply beautiful! Definitely eye candy and she knew exactly how to flaunt her perfect 36-24-38 frame. Her black complexion was glorious, radiant, and fierce. She was simply black and beautiful! She broke his staring spell, "Let me give you a tour of the rest of the house." She lived in a beautiful three bedroom house, with two levels and an attic. She had two and half bathrooms, one which was in her master bedroom. Wall to wall red carpet and his and hers closets with mirrored doors. Looking around her bedroom, he wanted to lounge there; it was very sensual and comfortable. She had a king size canopy bed with red, sheer fabric draping the bed. A 42' inch flat screen TV with surround sound and a play station attached. She showed him her bedroom as if she was saying; you better do your best to make it to this level. She led him back downstairs and they sat in the kitchen to talk.

erica was the Queen of her castle and any man who couldn't prove to her that he has royalty in his blood, couldn't be capable of being her King, especially in her castle where she makes the rules. She started her test in the kitchen to see how his conversation went face to face. She was more focused on getting to know one another and what the person is about. erica sat there with a penetrating stare not saying a word; Lagant felt that if he froze up, he wouldn't be there to long. He started the conversation off, "I know you get a lot of compliments on your smile—it's so beautiful!" "Some." "What makes it so pretty is how your sexy full lips spread— exposing your pearly whites and how it causes your dimples to sink in deeper. Your smile is very sincere—it seems as if you're always happy— By sitting here looking into your eyes, I can see that you're a vey serious lady." "You can tell that by looking in my eyes— really?" "Yes!" "Well, what else can you tell?" "I know the eyes are the window to your soul, and there's a reflection in your eyes of your feelings—I can tell that you still have that innocent girl in you, a girl who doesn't want to give up on love. I can tell that you protect your heart by any means necessary. Your eyes have the sight of freedom, free to be open with a person that you can trust. And you have a lot to share and a lot of love to give. Only you haven't found that freedom yet, but you do keep hope alive." He continued talking, trying to impress her.

Her smile turned into a face of a student; she was studying his statement; he was killing her softly with his words and reading her like a book. He seemed to be intelligent; she thought to herself; he had passed her first level. She asked, "Would like something to drink or eat." "I'm good on the food—but what do you have to drink?" "I have Pepsi, Kool-aid, orange juice and cold water." "You don't have anything stronger?" "No, I don't think so—wait the only thing close to strong is this bottle of champagne." "Ok that's good, let's put it on ice and celebrate!" "Celebrate?—Celebrate what?" "The start of our new friendship." She reached in the cabinet for the bottle and said, "Let's move into the living room." Lagant grabbed the bottle and made a toast, "God Bless this bottle of champagne that we're about to share in celebration of our new found friendship—No matter what the outcome is in the future, let us remain friends." As they walked into the front room. "Why did you do that?" "That's how you bless the bottle and hopefully it will bless our friendship also."

their personal lives and different life experiences that they had both been through. They talked about what they were looking for and expected in a relationship. "Through my experience, the most successful relationships are based on lies and deceit, and me personally, I can't deal with either. Honesty is the best policy; I just don't understand why men lie about some of the smallest things." "May be because we don't want to hurt you," "I'm just saying let me have the opportunity to make the choice if I want to either put up with it, or reject it." She took a sip of champagne, shaking her head and continued, "If a guy cheats he figures the woman should automatically forgive him. But when a woman cheats the guy is ready to kill her! I just don't understand the double standards." "Well, I, as a man; if my lady allows another guy to enter her sexually—then she was never mine—I'd feel like he had personally conquered my land and that she wasn't on my side. That makes her the enemy—that's why I think a lot of guys be ready to kill. Me, I'm a man of integrity. And I believe in morals and ethical principles. I'm not saying that I'm perfect. But if I have a strong woman who can understand me; and her love can put up with my wrongs; and she is willing to work with me; I know she would make me a better man." "Well, it's a thin line between love and hate. That's why when someone crosses that line with me, I can't take them back—I feel that he doesn't have respect for me as his woman nor his lover—God made Adam and eve! Not Adam, eve, and eva and the rest of the women for one man." "I understand you, but did it ever cross your mind, 'hypothetically speaking' why are there more women than men in the world?" "No! That doesn't have anything to do with a committed relationship. You trying to make excuses—A relationship is based on love, honesty, loyalty, trust, understanding and so much more!" "Not trying to be funny, but you did say understanding?—right, so let me ask you why wouldn't you understand your man if he slipped and had sex with another woman?" "You just don't slip into a woman, I don't care how drunk you claim to be and you knew exactly what you were doing!" erica was standing firm. She was not trying to compromise. Now Lagant was looking more like the student, as erica continued. "When you really love somebody, you want the best for that person; you don't want to dishonor them in anyway. They become a reflection of you. When other people see you they see your better half—you become one. Its not about just you anymore, it's about each other—love is a beautiful thing—It shouldn't turn you cold, bitter, revengeful or make you want to kill. Love shouldn't hurt. Love is kind; it doesn't envy— You must understand love before you tell someone you love them."

erica had Lagant thinking hard. He was thinking about real love that goes with a committed relationship. He tried to love Jada but was disappointed in her and it made him give up on love. But he knew that real love existed. He could see and hear it in erica, even though she had been hurt by love. She was wiser than he thought; she dropped a drink of love on him that he wasn't ready to hear. "So, you do believe in love?" Lagant asked, "Yes I believe in love. So many people have been deceived by the devil; they have given up on love. But with God in your life you will know that love never fails."

The whole love conversation was too much for Lagant's young ears; they talked and drank the bottle away. "I haven't drunk like this in a long time, I feel a little buzz." "I know you're not tipsy? That was nothing but champagne—flavored water—we need something just a little stronger to continue our celebration—Do you drink Alize?" "Yes, I have before, but where are you going to get it from?" "The liquor store, I'll be back in 30 minutes." erica's facial expression changed, she was starting to enjoy his company. "No! You don't have to go, we don't need to drink to celebrate." "Then how are we going to finish celebrating?" "I don't know but I know we can figure something out."

erica stood up and grabs him by the arm and brought him closer to her; he could smell her sweet smelling perfume. He looked her in the eyes, "I have a small bottle of Alize in the car, and I'll be back—two second style." He leaned down and pecked her lips; she smiled, liking their first contact. "You were fooling with me all that time (She leaned over and returned the peck back to his lips) you knew you had it in the car." She watched as he walked out to the car and returned with a bottle of Alize Red. "I've never had the red before." "Red must be our favorite color?" "You right!"

Lagant knew that she would be loose after this bottle. "Tastes good!" "So, you like the Red?" "Yes, (erica toasted. She raised the bottle then said) I bless this bottle to God—this is the blood to our friendship." Lagant raised his glass, "to blood!"—erica—I almost forget the reason why I'm here." "I'm not the reason you came over?" "Of course—but I almost forgot—I needed to help you pronounce my name correctly." "I did stutter your name, I'm sorry. I've never heard a name like yours before, it's so different but masculine." He told her to look at his lips and tongue as he pronounced his name over and over. She was looking at his mouth and loved how sexy his lips looked; she imagined his tongue licking her kitty cat.

His tongue trick seemed to be working. She was getting closer and closer to his face as she pronounced his name with him. He stared at her wet glossy lips and her tongue movement. They locked lips and started to kiss very passionately, they could feel each others body heat. "Did I get it right?" "I don't know, kiss me again and I'll let you know." They kissed again; erica began to moan while his hands wander all over her plump ass. She loved how his large hands were rubbing her. She liked how solid his body felt. He took both his hands and grip under her ass checks as if he was parting the red sea, thinking to himself—this is a lot of ass! He felt the warmth and wetness coming from between her. His blood start rushing through his body and he became hard instantly. She felt "it" growing bigger and getting harder against her stomach. They were breathing hard and heavy. They were in the heat of the moment. He slowly led her to the couch and gently sat her down. He lifts her halter top exposing her bare breast. Her nipples were hard and breasts were firm. He rubbed, licked, kissed and sucked on them like they were his favorite flavor candy. He was driving her crazy, he found her spot without even knowing; she wrapped her legs around his body and he could feel her pussy on fire. erica had an orgasm from the caressing of her breasts. He placed both of his hands on each side of her waist, gripping her black tights while sliding her panties off at the same time. He spread her legs apart and went to work eating her pussy. She was shivering, squirming and moaning in passion; he knew it was a green light. As he started to get undressed his phone started to vibrate. He thought that he put it on silent in the car; he was praying that she didn't notice. The vibration startled erica, bringing her back to earth from Venus. "Are you going to answer your phone?" "No, it's not important." He started back kissing on her stomach and rubbing her breasts, at the same time trying to cut the ringer off. His phone starting vibrating again and messed up the whole mood. erica got up, "Answer your phone!!!—I have to use the ladies room anyhow." Lagant sat on the couch, with his dick harder than evil, looking at the unknown number with the two new messages, thinking, "Damn!—what the fuck!"

The Waiting Game

Victoria sat at T.G.I.F's bar eating a chicken salad while the men there tried to get with her left and right. She was very polite; she accepted their drinks and conversation but kept it at that level. She passed on getting their phone numbers, but they weren't giving up. She thought to herself; "I do want a booty call, just not with any of these pricks. I'm waiting on my Black Knight." She was enjoying the attention though. She was the sexiest chick at the bar; the women there were rolling their eyes in jealousy. One lady was so envious, she walked over and introduced herself then sarcastically said, "I think its time for you to leave. I know what type of stank you are; you think you're perfect, coming in here dressed all provocatively and trying to appear innocent—You aint nothing but a home wrecker!" Victoria turned her back on the woman whom then turned her stool back around. "I'm not finished with you yet, Ms. High Almighty! Do you think you can take our husbands and break up our happy homes?" Victoria was getting upset; she knew the woman was to drunk but she wasn't going to continue to sit there and let her openly disrespect her. "Answer me bitch!" Victoria was furious, she took the drink one of the men had bought her and threw it in the drunken bitch's face. The woman stood there shocked, with vodka and orange juice running down her face onto her clothes; security rushed over and quickly escorted the mad woman away. The woman was still yelling, "You're what I call the lowest type of whore there is!"

One of the men asked Victoria was she ok. "Yes, can I have one of your cigarettes?" She didn't smoke but she needed something to calm her nerves. She sat there smoking and choking. She was upset the drunken lady had pulled her card. She didn't know her like that to be talking to her that way. The guys were still trying to talk to her, but she wasn't paying them any attention. She decided it was time to call Lagant; she excused herself and went to the restroom. She called and it rung and went to voicemail. She was at a loss for words; she hadn't planned on leaving a message. She managed to mumble his name only; she called right back. *"Hello— Lagant, this is Victoria, well Ms. Parker the nurse—we met at the hospital the other day. I'm at T.G.I.F in Portsmouth. If you could, I'd like for you to join me—I promise it would be worth your time. If you can't make it please call me back—I'm calling from my cell—I'm waiting on you!"* She was disappointed that he didn't answer his phone either time but she kept hope alive.

Sexual Healing

erica didn't have to use the ladies room, she only told Lagant that so she could collect her thoughts. She looked in the mirror and thought, "What am I doing?" She did need some sexual healing but she didn't want a one night stand. She knew that guys who get sex on the first day consider the girl easy and loose, but he had her open. (She shook her head) Damn! No man has ever come this close to getting my cookies on the first date; young buck definitely has the potential to wear the crown. The way he ate me out, he could be King of my throne; but first I must find out does he have any concubine's. She wanted him just as bad as he wanted her. But, before she gave up her royal jewels, all her curiosities would be answered first.

Lagant was waiting, patiently sipping his Alize and wondering if he could heat things back up with erica again. She walked back into the room and turned the dim lights to bright and cut off the stereo. "Did you handle your phone call?" "No, they must have dialed the wrong number, I didn't know the number." "You didn't want to find out who it was?" "I don't call back numbers that I don't know." "Well, why did you answer my call? You didn't know my number." "I was hoping, and wishing that you called—so I was expecting an unknown number." She looked at him side ways as to say, you expect me to believe that. He stood up and took the last swallow of his Alize, "All I kept thinking about was your pretty smile." He walked to her and rubbed her back, "Look at that sunshine smile, I needed to see it again."

She leaned in and kissed him on the lips, she thought he was so sweet. He thought she wanted to get it popping again. "I'm sorry Lagant, it's getting late and I need to get some rest for work tomorrow morning." He stood there crushed; all hopes of smashing Buffy the Body went down the drain. "I understand, you got to get ready to be Ms. Cotton." She noticed a sad look come across his young face; she gave him a hug and a small kiss. "That sounds good—I'll see you soon."

As he sat in the car, he checked his messages to see who was blowing up his cell phone. To his surprise it was Ms. Parker. "Oh shit—da nurse!—Your call messed it up for me with erica—I couldn't get Buffy the Body, but the white Serena Williams will do! She must want to operate on me; she could start with my blue balls—He laughs out. Thank God it's Friday's!—I'm on my way!"

Lagant was doing 85 mph down the freeway. When he pulled into the parking lot, it was so packed, he was fortunate to find a spot. He called Victoria to let her know he was outside. "Ms. Parker, I got your message, I'm out front of T.G.I.F now." Victoria insisted that he come in. She wanted to make sure that he gets a couple of drinks in his system. "I'm sitting at the bar—do you want me to order you anything to eat?" "Yeah, get me a cheese burger with fries—wait—no ketchup!" "Ok, come on in!"

When he walked into the bar area every stool was occupied with mostly white people. He stood there looking for her. She walked up to him; he didn't even recognize her. She looked like a model from King's Magazine, with her stilettos on she was standing eye to eye with him. He knew she was pretty but she took the cake. Lagant damn near melted when she hugged and kissed him. "There you are, come on." He watched her fierce walk as she led him to the bar. every step she made in her red stiletto made him want to become her sex slave. He thought to himself, "She acts like we're the best of friends, she must be a freak." He sat down and ordered his favorite drink, a Long Island Ice Tea. He orders that because it helps him get there faster and it brings out his "A" game. But most of all, it helps him with his stamina to perform like a stallion when he's in action (sex-wise). Victoria ordered two Ice Teas, even though she never had it before. Lagant started eating his food while they watched the bartender mix there drinks. "That's a lot of liquor!" "Yes it is, and you have to drink it." "Don't worry I will—you think I can't do it—watch." She sipped it, "It tastes good, and you can't even taste the liquors." "How long you been here?" "Not long, a couple of hours."

They made small talk while Lagant continued to eat. She was becoming more intoxicated as she continued to drink more of her drink. She started to open up to him. (She slurred her words as she spoke.) "I don't want any problems with your baby's mother—I know you told me that you're not with her—But I don't want to come between what you two have going on—I do think your sexy, I wanted you when I first saw you—I don't usually do things like this—but it's something about you that's drawn me to you—I haven't stopped thinking about you since we first met." She leaned over and whispered in his ear. "That same night I masturbated thinking about you" She told him everything, from the champagne to the bubble bath. He was aroused by what she was saying and how her words tickled his ear. Victoria had one hand on his leg and the other around his shoulder; she had the young stallion ready for action. He told her he was ready to leave and she thought he meant leave her behind. "You ready to leave me, don't leave, let me buy you one more drink." "No thanks, we both have had too much—I don't want to leave you I want to leave with you. Let's go somewhere more private." "Oh, alright!—let's go—we can go to my house, there's enough privacy there." "What are we waiting for?"

He grabbed her hand and led the way through the crowd. The guy that was previously keeping her company saw them and thought. "I'm not letting this nigga leaving with her, especially after I've been working on her all night!" He stopped Victoria by grabbing her shoulder. "Hey Victoria, are you alright?" "Oh Hi—yes, I'm good. I'm about to leave—It was nice to meet you." Lagant stood there patiently waiting, still holding her hand. "Why don't you stay, I'll make sure you make it home." "No thank you." She wrapped her arm around Lagant, "My friend is here." The guy frowned then said, "Who is this nigga!" Lagant was still holding on to Victoria's hand while with the other, he took his hand and punched the guy across his chin, knocking the guy smooth on his ass. "Let's get the fuck out of here!" Lagant yelled, "Can you drive?" "Yes." "I'm going to follow you, Ok?"

They made it to Victoria's house in twenty minutes. As they were driving he started to see more and more big and tall trees everywhere. The streets turned darker, Street lights became farther away, just as the houses did. When Lagant saw the big brick house in the secluded, wooded area, he knew she had a lot of dead presidents. {That's money} She parked in front of the house; he followed and parked behind her. It looked like he was in a different world. The air seemed to be fresher; the stars were bigger and brighter. "You live here by yourself?" She smiled and wrapped her arms around him, "My daughter is off to college—It's just me and my dog—do you like it?" "Hell yeah!—I love it! What kind of dog do you have?" "A pit-bull named Bones—he's harmless, you don't have to worry about him." She turned the key to open the door. Bones barked.

"Whoa—wait, I didn't come here to meet your dog—you have to put him up!" She cracked the door and held the dog by his collar while Lagant tried to walk in. Bones started barking uncontrollably. "Hold him!" Bones was jerking and pulling away, trying to get at Lagant. She was too drunk to hold him. Lagant started stepping back once he noticed that she was having problems holding him. Bones broke her grip and Lagant hauled ass. He ran so fast, he was able to jump on top of her SUV with Bones right behind him barking and jumping on the SUV trying to get Lagant. She snapped the leash and pulled him away, locking Bones to the tree. "I'm sorry Lagant; he usually doesn't act like this." She'd never had company over before to know how Bones would react; she always assumed he was a friendly dog. Lagant looked at Victoria then said, "Just because he's friendly with you, doesn't mean he's like that with everybody else." He slowly jumped off her SUV and they went into her house. He looked around in amazement. The living room was spacious with a large, brick fireplace and a large crystal chandelier. The floors were oak wood with throw rugs covering some areas. everything in it seemed to be new. "Damn!—you have a really nice house." "Thank you, I'm glad that you like it, I'll give you a tour another time right know I'm going to show you my bedroom!"

She grabbed his hand and led him upstairs to the master bedroom. Victoria was happy that her plan didn't fail. This was the night she had been preparing for. She sat him on her king size water bed and took off his Nike's. "Get comfortable." He laid back enjoying the comfort of her water bed while she turned on the CD player and made things a little more cozier. He was watching her every move. He was still a little spooked by Bones; he started thinking crazy thoughts about Ms. Parker; the nurse by day, killer freak by night—he couldn't understand how could she live in this big ass house by herself? He thought she probably does this with other guys and they turn up missing, and or bury their bones in the woods or even feeds them to her crazy ass dog Bones; I hope this bitch is not setting me up on some KKK shit? This bitch might just be crazy, why do she want me, knowing that I just had a baby by one of her patients—I'm glad I brought my gun with me. Let her try some stupid shit and it's going to be a lot of dead ass crackers up in here!"

Through all his negative thoughts, he was still able to stay focused on sexing Victoria. His last thought before Victoria got his full attention was; "Chasing pussy one day is going to be my down fall. (He looked at her as she started to perform.) If sex is a sin may God forgive me?" Victoria was stripping off her clothes piece by piece and slow dancing to the music very seductively. every piece that she took off she swung like a helicopter blade and tossed each item at him. She was exposing her firm titties, her nipples were erect. She grabbed her breasts pushed them together, while sticking her tongue out trying to lick on her nipples. Then she untied her scarf that she wore as a belt and slid it out while shaking her hips from side to side and turning around slowly, showing him her ass. She slapped her ass causing it to bounce, then looked back at Lagant and blew a kiss. He was enjoying her performance and was already aroused by her sexual dance; she bent over poking her heart shaped ass out and looked at him threw her legs. She was telling him that she liked it from the back, her titties bounced as she moved the scarf back and forth through her thighs as if she was sexing it. She unbuttoned her pants and swarmed out of them, letting them fall to the floor, showing off her red thongs; he watched on in excitement. He was floating on the water bed as he started to stroke his manhood keeping it at attention. She walked closer to him. He watched as her hips swayed from side to side, dressed only in her red thong and red stilettos. Lagant raised his body up but she lifted her foot and gently put her heel on his chest laying him back down. "Relax."

She straddled his legs while pulling down his pants just enough to expose his rock hard penis. She wastes no time, she started licking him like she had an ice cream cone in front of her. And she was bobbing her head and making all kinds of slurping sounds. He had bust off fast from being so horny. He laid there breathing heavy with his toes curled. "Did you like it?" "That was fucking great!" "The best is yet to come!" She went into the bathroom and turned on the shower; she then lit the scented candles and turned off the lights. "Come join me!" Lagant took off all his clothes, stashed his gun on the floor under the nightstand and quickly joined her. She was rinsing soap off of her body; she then took the soap and started to wash his body. All they could see was their silhouettes. He gripped her firm ass and his manhood was back rock hard again. She could feel it on her stomach; she turned around putting her hands on the wall and arched her back. She looked very exotic with the shower water running down her body from head to toe. Lagant entered her with no hesitation. She was so wet and hot on the inside, her pussy was pulsating and he loved how tight it was. He could tell that she hadn't been touched by a man for a long time; she was screaming in ecstasy as he entered her. She yelled his name over and over, she could feel him all in her stomach and he rode her like a bull.

She manage to say "My pussy belongs to you, promise that you will take care of it?" "I got you!" "I love the way you're fucking me—oww Lagant fuck me!" "You love this dick!" "I do—I do oow Lagant!" "Give me my pussy then!" They were fucking like maniacs as the shower water ran down their bodies. "Oh shit! I'm about to cum—oooh Lagant!" He felt her pussy throbbing. "Baby I'm about to nut!" His body became so tense he was pumping off beat, "Give it to me baby!" His body muscles flexed. "Oh shit! Oh shit, there it goes!" His body seemed to go paralyzed as he nutted inside of her. He was still holding on to her, grinding until he was all the way finished. They stayed in that position panting and holding each other. Once they calmed down she turned and kissed him, then they got out the shower. She handed him a towel to dry off. He watched as she dried the glistening water off of her sexy frame. She put on a pink silk robe and escorted him back into the bedroom. She grabbed the Grey Goose and poured them a shot. She looked him in the eyes, and said "I'm not finished with our sex escapade just yet!"

Jada's Guilt

Jada had just finished feeding Iesha her last bottle for the night. She was burped, changed, washed up and ready for bed. It took Iesha fifteen minutes and she was off to sleep, smiling in her dreams. Jada placed her in her crib and watched her sleep, until her mind was sidetracked by negative thoughts. Jada thought, by getting herself a younger man, she would be able to mold him into the man she wanted him to be. But everything seemed to be back firing on her. She felt responsible for the way Lagant was reacting to her. She didn't want to think she was a bad person for putting her son up for adoption; she lay on their bed staring at the empty spot that Lagant should've been occupying. She was missing him more now than ever before; she held the pillow in her arms and started to cry. She hoped that he would call. He usually did when he stayed out pass his usual time; she felt that things were changing between them. She had visions of him having sex with other women in their bed while she was in the hospital. She wondered if he had met someone new and where he really was tonight. She found it hard to believe that he was celebrating with Tino. She knew that Lagant was young, fine, charming and had the ability to make even a married woman curious.

Jada didn't want to feel guilty for what her mother forced her to do; it was either give her son up for adoption or have an abortion. She didn't want to abort the life that was growing inside of her so she chose to give life. It was as though her pass was now haunting her; if only she had the courage to fight against her mother, she would have her son. Jada cried even more. All her pain was coming out. She felt that Lagant's love for her was quickly drifting away. She thought to herself "Is it best that I let Gant grow into the man he is made out to be?" She liked him for his qualities and loved him, even his defects. But she also loved him enough to let him go. If it was meant to be, she knew that it would be; and he would return to her. She unlocked her dairy and wrote down the events of the day. If Jada only knew that the nurse she confided in had schemed on her and now had her man in her bed of lace, belly to belly, face to face, mouth full of tongue, hands full of fun; Lagant and Victoria too drunk to cum!

Khalil's Plan

Khalil called Cool Breeze and told him to meet him at his baby's mother's house. Cool Breeze wasted no time arriving. Khalil told him about his plan and that he paid half on Rock's lawyer. He let him know that he was on his was to Virginia to lay low from parole and the real reason he wanted talk to him. "What's popping Blood?" "Before I leave I need to take care of the snitch that put me behind bars! This is personal; I just need someone who got the wheel." This was the day Khalil had dreamed about, he could taste the blood in his mouth.

Larry Smith— the by stander who witnessed the shooting of Michael Scott by him. Larry thought he was being a good citizen by taking the stand and pointing out Khalil to the jury. Khalil had replayed that day over and over again in his mind. He vowed that one day he would put Larry 6 feet under for taking ten years of his life away. Larry didn't have any idea that the defendant gets a copy of the entire transcript when they take their case all the way to trial. Khalil knew all of Larry's information like the back of his hands. It was now or never. Khalil knew that the police would catch up with him one day for his violation but he was going to make it hard for them.

Larry lived his life as a good citizen. He was married with two children that were grown, one married and the other off in college. Larry owned a laundry matt on So. Orange Ave in Newark call Suds r Us. It was the same laundry matt that Khalil shot Michael Scott in front of. Larry thought he was a Good Samaritan by cooperating with the police. But in the streets he was considered nothing but a snitch, and snitches get ditches. Larry had no idea that one day he would be a victim of revenge. While he and his wife lay in bed cuddling, the door bell rang.

Doggie Style

Lagant stretched his arms out and yawned, it was 4am. "Victoria it's been great but my night is over with." "No, no! Please stay!" She rubbed her hand across his chest, feeling his skin. "I'll cook you a hot breakfast in the morning, whatever you want." "That sounds great but I'll have to take a rain check on that." Lagant thought to himself, "She wants me to get comfortable and go to sleep; so when I wake up, I'll be tied up somewhere." "Let me get my black ass out of here." She started rubbing his manhood; "But I'm not finished." She reached over and pulled out a bottle of K-Y jelly then slid from between the black satin sheets and bent over in a doggie style position. She rubbed the K-Y all over her ass while looking back at him, "I want you to have all of me, I'm giving you my most special prize—It's never been touched, it's yours—baby, please be gentle."

Lagant instantly became erect looking at her oiled heart shaped ass. He reached in his pants, grabbed a condom and slid it on. All those thoughts of the KKK went out the window; he got close to her and positioned himself. "easy baby." She could feel the large bulge trying to make its way into her small canal. He was so excited, he couldn't get it in; he was trying to force it in. "Don't hurt me baby." That was exactly what he wanted to do! He never had anal sex before; this was a first for both of them. every time he got the head of his dick in her, she would jump forward, "Oh!—Wait baby—wait!" He replied anxious. "Relax baby and don't move!" He started taking his time and sweet talking her through it; his stimulating words calmed her down, she started to moan. Before she knew it he was in her, she gave off a loud moan that sounded more like a cat crying. As he penetrated her she felt a feeling that she had never felt before, it was like when she first got her cherry popped. Victoria buried her head into the sheets and arched her back and moaned like a virgin.

Once he got his whole penis inside, he started to stroke like there was no tomorrow. She yelled, "It hurt!" She tried to twist and break loose of his grip, but he had a tight grip on her. She had to take the pleasure punishment that he was giving her, that she welcomed him to. He wasn't letting up on her; he was putting his back into it! As time pass, she started to get into it and began to wiggle her body back and forth. He reached around and started finger fucking her, she started talking in tongues. He couldn't understand a word she was saying, she was growling and shaking her head wildly. His hands were soaking wet from her multiple orgasms. Lagant couldn't hold back, his body began to flex, and then he released himself. He picked her up and flipped her body on top of his like she was on a roller coaster ride. This was a ride neither one of them would forget. They laid back. She starts placing small kisses on his face; with every kiss she whispered, "Thank you baby—that felt different but it was great!" Lagant laid there breathing heavily as if he just got finished lifting weights.

The Hit

Larry's wife Barbara asked, "Who could that be at this hour?" "I don't know honey, I'm not expecting anyone." The door bell rung again. "I'm going down stairs to see who it could be." He looked at the time, it was 10:45 pm; he put on his slippers and pajama top. "Baby you lay there—I'll be right back." When Larry reached the front door he became suspicious and grabbed the bat out of the closet. He looked through the peep hole but it was too dark to see anything. Khalil was ahead of his game; he had unscrewed the light bulb. Larry peeked again before he said anything. He could only see a shadow.

Khalil had revenge on his mind; he leaned on the bell harder. He wore no mask, only black fitted gloves, it was personal. And he wanted Larry to see who was going to turn him into a ghost. Khalil was going to kill everybody in the house if need be, he wasn't leaving any witnesses. Larry became annoyed, "Who is it?" Khalil had a flashback when he heard the voice; he took his fully loaded desert eagle and placed it to the peep hole then pulled the trigger. The bullet broke through the heavy wooden door hitting Larry in the side of the neck, causing him to fall to the floor; Barbara jumped out of bed frightened by the sound and called out for Larry.

Khalil shot the door lock off and kicked the door open. Barbara went for the phone; she knew she heard shots for sure. Khalil saw Larry lying on the floor holding his neck, Khalil stood over him looking him in his eyes. Larry laid there with his eyes wide open as if he had just seen a ghost. He tried to talk but not a word came out of his mouth. Khalil shot a bullet straight through Larry's mouth, then kicked him. "I bet you won't be snitching out of that any more." He looked around, the house was empty, and he tucked his gun and put on his hood and was out the front door.

Speedy had already pulled the car up in front of the house, Khalil jumped in and they were off. Barbara was in the room, soaked in her own urine, she wanted to get the phone she dropped but was too scared to move. She thought the gunman was coming for her next. Until she heard tires squeal; she looked out the window and saw a black car pulling off.

Speedy was the best car thief in the hood; everybody knew about his skills. They were almost on Route 280 heading east when he sped through the red light. South Orange police were in the cut. The cops turned on their cherry top lights and were approaching them fast. Speedy was driving a black convertible sport coupe Ferrari Spyder. The police had just received the call of a shooting on Day Street, on their radio. They police radioed in for back-up; they were now on 280 dipping in and out of traffic. "Damn!" Khalil yelled out. He pulled out his desert eagle and took it off safety. "Don't worry blood, I got the wheel. Watch my work!" Khalil wasn't trying to go back to jail, "Lose them motherfuckers!" Speedy fish tailed, dipping in and out of traffic; the cops couldn't keep up with him. He had a six car lead on them by the time the traffic moved out the way for the police. Speedy had a straight away with no cars in sight. He shifted the clutch into fifth gear. When the cops made it through, all they could see were the tail lights of the Ferrari disappearing over the hill. They never got a chance to get a good look at the license plates.

Shakur Reprimand

As security locked the door behind the last party goers it was 2:00 am and all the workers at the Moonlight hustled, cleaning and straightening up the club. Starlette closed out all the cash registers and gathered all the work receipts then did inventory. Shakur was in his office doing a final count of the day's business earnings. He separated the work orders from his side hustle. The Moonlight did great for the day, they grossed $8,000. Starlette watched as he put the money into the hidden safe that's in his office. Then he gave her the checks to pay his employees and looked over his work orders. He noticed one order request for a late night delivery from his main man Mel; he placed it in the stack with the other orders and placed them in his briefcase.

He locked the office door and went to the front; everyone was finished working and the club looked like it was never occupied with party goers. They sat around and talked about the different situations they observed earlier in the night. Shakur thought that one of them had witnessed what happened between him and Lagant. But his mind was just playing tricks on him; instead they were cheering him on about what happen with the car thieves. "They didn't know he had fight game in him like that." He smiled waving them off, "Go head—ya'll crazy." They continued to tease him while reenacting the scene, he locked the door and they all said their goodbyes.

As he drove Starlette home, he knew it would be a good time to talk and catch up with her. He wanted to know more about her mystery man, "you know the line of business we in Star; we have to be careful who we date." "Shakur—you say that to say what?—Say what you mean and don't beat around the bush!—Besides what line of business are you talking about?—Because all I do is manage a club!" "Star you know I have so much going on—I don't want no one playing you close and trying to infiltrate me—honestly, I don't want him around you!—you know how I feel about those service guys." Starlette sighed, "everyone that is in the service isn't like our father—Trust me!—Lagant may be from the hood but he's a good guy—he doesn't know about you or your drugs—I don't talk to him about your business—Shakur, your worrying about nothing! And if he breaks my heart, so be it! — We all go through that—Fuck it!—I'll heal!" "Star, I've been in this game for a long time and I can tell when a person has gone bad. How did your friend know that someone was breaking into your car, how you know it wasn't a set up-remember he left over 30 minutes earlier. Are you sure he didn't have anything to do with it?" "Come on Shakur—don't you think if he did, the car would have been gone; you saw the blood by the car, come on—what is it with you—you sound envious of him! And I don't know for what, you have so much more than he does." Shakur thought about it, he knew that he was out of place intruding in her personal affairs. He didn't want to admit it nor admire Lagant's swag. But he saw a lot of his self in Lagant, and he could tell that he was advanced for his age. "Star I hope that you're right about this guy. But if you're happy then I'm happy." They talked about this and that until he dropped her off, his night wasn't over yet. He drove to his hide away to package up his orders for tomorrow; he looked at his orders and realized that Mel wants five more keys, besides his usual five.

Wee hours of the Morning

Victoria had her arm wrapped around Lagant as they lay in bed recuperating from their sex-capades. every time he tried to move she would hold him tighter. "Don't leave yet, it's almost morning." He was staring at the ceiling thinking how she had just given him her body. He was feeling her sex style. He knew he had her wrapped physically, now he was ready to get into her mentally. But he was sticking with his first rule, 'don't get emotionally attached.' He figured she wanted to keep him there for a morning round of sex. He gently ran his fingers through her hair and started talking very smooth to her in a mellow voice. She became relaxed and fell soundly asleep, hugging him as if he was the last man on earth. Lagant eased out of her grip and swiftly put his clothes on, then wrote her a note.

> *Miss Victoria Parker, thank you for a wonderful night, I feel much better now that you've operated on me. I'm not trying to be disrespectful, but I think we made a mistake. I think it's better if we don't see each other know more ! Please don't call. Sorry . . .*

Lagant arrived home early in the morning, Jada was sound asleep, and he noticed a green book that was unzipped lying next to her. He gently picked it up and discovered it was a diary. He never knew that she kept a diary. His curiosity got the best of him, he figured now was the perfect opportunity to discover anything else that she was hiding. The diary was open on,

July 29 1992

> *Dear Diary: I can feel Gant slowly slipping away; I knew something like this would happen. Maybe it's my fault for not being honest with him about my son; I never wanted him to find out— especially the way that he did. He has every right to be upset with me, I feel like I'm taking him through too much for him to be a young man. I don't want to destroy his innocence; I know that he tried hard to love me. But I've always made it difficult for him, stupid me just wanting to be loved too badly! I have no right to put him through this anguish because of my selfishness, but I really do love him and I don't want to lose him. I don't know what I would do if he ever found out what happened nine months ago. I hate myself for it; if it wasn't for Iesha, I'd kill myself! Somebody help me! God help me!*

Lagant didn't know what to think; he believed Jada needed some professional help at times, but he got stuck on what she meant by (what happened nine months ago). He slowly turned the pages, going back into Jada's pass; he thought, 'nine months ago; that's when Jada had conceived. He was confused? She must hate herself for becoming pregnant; this bitch didn't want to have my baby?!' (As he turned through the pages) He was becoming more anxious and furious . . . .

May 20, 1992

> *Dear Diary: I don't feel attractive; I know that Gant says I look good, but his ass just wants some pussy. Can't he see that I'm seven months pregnant; how could he want to have sex? Sometimes I wish he was older! Just because I don't open my legs for him, he's upset. It's been two months now since we've had sex and I'm not planning on having any until after the baby is born. Long as I have Maria, I'm good; so be mad Mr. Man!*

"This bitch deprived me of sex and she had the nerve to be fucking the same girl she sent to test my loyalty; and she's bragging about it! I wasn't mad; I was horny you stinking bitch. Now I'm fucking mad!" let me see what else this bitch wrote in here!

April 11, 1992

Dear Diary: I went to the doctor today and I found out that I'm having a baby girl! Yes! I'm so excited! Gant doesn't know the sex yet. I know he wants a boy but I pray that he's happy with a girl.

January 5, 1992

Dear Diary: It's official; I'm nine weeks pregnant; the test was accurate. I'm so afraid, not sure if I'm ready to be a mother. But no matter what, I'm not aborting or considering adoption. My pain comes from not knowing if Gant's my baby's father. I pray to God that Gant is the father of my child. I calculated the time and it leads back to when Gant went out to sea for that week. And I had a surprise visitor.

Lagant's eyes were wide open; he remembered going out to sea with the USS Albany back in October. He was out for a promotional ceremony. He had made rank and the USS Albany was one of his accounts. They wanted to show him their appreciation, so they invited him aboard the submarine for a week. That was their way of rewarding him for his dedication and hard work. And his new rank as e-5. It was one of the best experiences he'd ever had. He knew Jada was acting funny when he returned home from his cruise. He was rushing wanting to read more of Jada's diary. He turned the pages but it stopped. That was the beginning of the diary. He began to pace the floor. His mind was racing, he started pacing faster and faster, "this secretive, slut ass bitch! She's been using me all this time, playing with my feelings and emotions like I'm stupid! Iesha has to be mine! What would I tell my family?"

Lagant was hurt and disappointed. He became furious and wanted to kill Jada himself. He grabbed a knife and walked into their bedroom. With red eyes, he could taste blood in his mouth and murder was on his mind! He put the knife to Jada's neck. Tears were falling from his eyes like water from a faucet. He wasn't in his right state of mine. Jada was stretched out on the bed sleeping, to him she no longer looked like the woman he first fell in love with nor his baby mother. Lying there, she looked like a piece of shit! As bad as he wanted to kill her, he couldn't do it. He thought about Iesha. He walked back to the kitchen and vomited in the sink. He fell to the floor and stabbed the knife into the floor. "I should kill her!"

God must have sent an angel to save Jada and to comfort him. He slowly regained his composure. He cleaned up his mess and placed the diary back on the bed just as he had found it. He went into Iesha's room. She was awake in her crib looking like she was lost in la-la land. "Tell me you my daughter?" She looked at him with those innocent baby's eyes as if to say—you know you're my father! "Daddy's sorry baby, it's not our fault, baby. I have to find out the truth. Your mother is full of secrets and lies. She would never have told me that she cheated. It's because of you; you saved your mother's life tonight— You have to be my daughter! Iesha, I promise you I will never lie to you like your mother did to me— It's my job to teach you all that I know, you are my future. even if you're not my blood, I will still be in your life as your father. And when you're old enough to understand, I promise I will tell you everything. Your mother's planning on teaching you all those falsehoods that America brain-washes kids into believing. I'm not going to let you think there's a Santa Claus; they try to cover up the true meaning of Christmas with a fat white man in a red outfit. You will know the real meaning; it's a Christian holiday celebration of the birth of God's only begotten Son, Jesus. The Chosen One. And it's not even his correct birth day. Then to make it worse, they cover up his death and resurrection with a snow bunny calling it easter— Baby don't worry, I got your back, this world is crazy— no, I mean the people in this world are crazy. There's so much to learn; all I want you to do is take your time and not rush to become grown, ok . . ." Iesha went fast to sleep listening to the sound of her father's voice. "That's my Boo." He placed her on his chest and lay back in his recliner and went to sleep.

Jada was up at 6:30 am, and noticing that she hadn't put her diary up, she quickly zipped and locked it. She stashed it and then went to check on the baby. She almost had a heart attack when Iesha wasn't in her crib. She didn't hear Lagant come in, so she started to panic; once she hit the living room and saw Iesha lying across his chest she was calm again. Her mind flashed to her diary being left out, she wondered how long he had been home? And why didn't he come to bed; she hoped that he hadn't read her diary. She loved how they looked sleeping. She went to get her camera for a quick picture and then she went into the kitchen to make Iesha a bottle.

She gently lifted Iesha off of Gant's chest and they both woke up feeling their bond separated. "Sssssh, mommy got you baby, don't cry; are you ready to eat?" Lagant looked at her with repugnance, he wanted to snap on her, but he remembered what his mother taught him. That the woman is the weaker sex never put your hands on her no matter what, or how upset you get. Hitting her would not make the problem go away; it will not make you any bigger of a man or more in charge—It makes things worse, you always have to use what God has given you, your mind; that's what makes you a man! The most powerful weapon and gift a man could have. (She would always end it with) Would you want a man to hurt me, your mother?" When he was younger he promised himself that he would never be a woman beater but this was the test of his life time.

He walked to their bedroom not saying a word. She watched as he walked and wanted to talk to him but she was scared and wasn't able to get the words out of her mouth. She didn't know what to say. She felt that he could now see through her or maybe he had read her diary. She chose not to say anything. She focused her full attention back to Iesha then started talking baby talk to her. She couldn't stop wondering whether or not he had read her diary; she figured if he did he would have said or did something to her by now. She thought of some of the contents in her diary, like Valentines Day. That was the day she gave him a box of chocolates shaped in a heart with a card. He gave her a 14 karat gold bracelet and took her out to an Italian restaurant. He treated her very special on the lover's holiday, when they returned home Lagant wanted to be romantic. She led him on, teasing him sexually. When he went to take off her clothes she shut him down, leaving him confused. "What's the problem?" "Gant, I'm really not in the mood; it's been a good day let's just hold each other." He became upset, "I'll be back." "Where are you going?" "I don't know, any place but here!" He walked out of the apartment and slammed the door; Jada laughed as he walked out. Later on that night Jada began to write in her diary. *"I masturbated tonight thinking of Tino, it's just something about him that turns me on, I think it's his hazel eyes."*

Jada prayed he didn't read her diary; she knew if he did, it would really be over.

Once Iesha was asleep, Jada jumped into the bed with Lagant and wondered what he was doing last night. He was sound asleep and snoring; she reached her hand around him placing her hand in his boxers. He jumped up, moved her hand, "Stop touching me, I'm trying to sleep!", and turned his back to her; she was only trying to do a smell check. It smelled fresh, so she didn't know what to think about his night out. Having him back in bed with her, she started reminiscing about their last sex sessions, and she became horny.

Lagant woke up around 12noon breaking Jada's hold she had on him, "What time is it?" He ignored her as they both got up out of bed doing their Saturday routines. Lagant went to shower; Jada followed him into the shower. She was trying to be the perfect girlfriend. He thought about elbowing her in the face and drowning her. He calmly washed his body; Jada soaked the sponge with peppermint soap and started washing his back while making small talk. She started to pry into his affairs from last night, "I don't want to talk about last night!" He snapped. "Are you ok?" She asked while still washing his back, "No, I'm not ok, I need time to myself, and we have to put our relationship on hold." "What do you mean on hold? We have a daughter together—it's a little too late to be on hold."

Lagant wanted to mention seeing her diary but he wanted to find out where she stashed the past years of her life. He knew that if he asked her she wouldn't be honest, he needed to see with his own eyes. "Jada, I'm still Iesha's father, she doesn't have anything to do with our situation." "Oh, now you want to break up?" Jada's voice escalated. "Jada, I need time alone." He washed the soap off his face and stepped out of the shower with Jada right behind him, still soapy. "Time!—Time for what Lagant? Time for you to find another family?" Lagant was ignoring her; she was persistent, "Answer me Lagant Mills!" every time she was upset she called him by his full name, he turned around looking directly into her eyes. "Jada we need space and you know why!" "I don't think we need space—for what!—You're talking about moving out?" "Yes!" His answer shocked and hurt her, tears flooded her eyes, and "You want to leave me and your daughter? I can't believe you want to leave us!"

Lagant wrapped the towel around his waist and went to the closet looking for something to wear while Jada sat on the bed asking the same questions over and over. "I'm not leaving my daughter." "Yes you are— you're leaving me and her!" She screamed and started punching the bed, he turned from the closet. He couldn't hold his tongue any longer. (In a harsh voice) "Jada I read your fucking diary, now tell me, is Iesha my daughter?! Or is it the guy you fucked in October!" Jada saw his muscles flex and the veins in his forehead and neck pop out; she knew he was furious. She remembered the last time he got that upset, it wasn't a pretty sight. She jumped up, ran into the bathroom and locked the door. "You don't have shit to say about that?!" All the noise woke Iesha; he paced in front of the door yelling. "You see what you did; you scared the baby!" "You need to let us know who her father is." "I'm sorry", was all she could say over and over again. "What!—you were planning on lying to us all of our lives?" "I know that you are Iesha's father!" "Tell me how you know; when you fucked another nigga—he could be the father! Tell me Jada—how long you been fucking him? Plus you on that lesbian shit! You expect me to believe you, every word comes out your mouth is a fucking lie—you are a fucking liar! You lied to me from the beginning!" "I Love you Gant, you're Iesha's father!" "Love me!—You didn't love me that night-anyway love aint have shit to do with DNA—I want a test! I need to know for myself!"

He went into Iesha's room and picked her up, "Don't cry baby girl, it's alright. Your mother and I are having a little quarrel, she's caught in a lie-as usual-but she can't get out of this one." He walked back to the bathroom door, "Jada, your daughter wants to know if I'm her father? Jada—I know you hear me! Jada—your diary says differently-look at that, you don't even know your damn self—Okay, then tell me who the other guy is, tell me?" "Gant, please stop it!" He laid the baby on the bed and started trashing Jada's things looking for her diary; she peeked out the bathroom door. "What are you doing?" "Where's your diary?—You're not going to tell me where it's at?" "Please Gant, stop this; why can't you believe me?" "Believe you—yeah right!—Come out the bathroom—why did you lock yourself in there? I'm not going to hit you."

Jada didn't chance it; she'd seen red in his eyes. She stayed in the bathroom while he got dressed. Lagant had to calm down, Jada was still scared. "Jada—it is what it is! I'm stepping out to get my mind right—you fucked me up! Call me when my brother calls—give him my cell phone number." He placed the baby in her crib and left, "Take care of your daughter. Jada slowly opened the door making sure that he was gone. She went to the window and saw his car pulling out of the parking lot. "I'm sorry Iesha but I know that Gant is your father, the DNA will prove it!" [We all know the saying; mother's baby, father's maybe??]

Another Day Another Dollar

Shakur was finished with all of his drop offs for the morning except for the kilos that his man Money Mel had ordered, which he requested be dropped off at 8pm. Shakur had been dealing with Mel for over five years; Mel had half of Portsmouth locked down. His usual order was 5 keys every two weeks, they did good business together. Shakur was the one who gave Melvin his nickname, Money Mel. Shakur helped Mel get started in the game. He liked how Mel had everybody in his hood respecting him. He started fronting Mel a kilo at a time, and Mel always would have his money correct. Over the years Mel had got his clientele up and he was copping 5 kilos every two weeks. Shakur figured Mel must have had a come up, ordering five extra keys this time.

He finished up and placed $20,000 in his drop floor safe and went to Nubians for some breakfast and to talk with his good friend Rashid. When he arrived at the Moonlight he saw his accountant's car parked bedside Star's truck. He forgot that he had an appointment with his accountant today. Shakur didn't want problems with the I.R.S, so he made sure all his taxes were paid up for all his businesses. His net pay went into his business account at Mutual Federal. They had it set up so his employees could have direct deposit if they liked. He made sure that in appearance he was a clean cut man on one hand, but on the other hand he was a kingpin in the drug game. Shakur had mastered the saying, "don't let your right hand know what your left hand is doing. He was a one man army.

Starlette walked into his office, "How were your deliveries?" "everything went smooth, I'm glad you asked because I'm going to need you to stay a little later tonight. I have to make a drop off to Money Mel at eight o'clock tonight." Star's eyes got wide and she thought to herself—I hope he doesn't take long. She had plans to spend some time with Lagant tonight. "I'm not going to be long." "I got you brother." "Good, I've got a lot of errands to handle today so I'm going to need you to hold it down here." "Don't I always?" "Yes, you do sis, and you're doing a great job. I don't know what I would do without you!" She smiled from ear to ear, his words made her feel needed and she was happy to be of help to him. Shakur walked over and gave her a kiss on the forehead and they walked to the bar area. everybody was there preparing their stations for the work day.

Disappointment

The sun was beaming through Victoria's sliding glass doors; the rays reached her eyes and caused the sleeping beauty to wake up. Her hazel eyes opened then closed quickly. Her head was pounding. She grabbed her head and thoughts of last night raced through her mind. She turned looking for her lover but saw that he wasn't there; she called out his name twice but no response. She tried to get out of bed when her womanly parts down below started to throb; it brought a smile to her face as she reminisced about the night. It had been a long time since she'd felt a man's touch, she felt like a teenager again. She stretched and looked around her bedroom; her thong was flung on the other side of the room, and she spotted a used condom on the floor. She laughed as she walked around in her birthday suit.

Victoria was feeling like eve in the garden thinking about her black Adam. She glances to look at the clock and sees a note from Lagant; as she read it she became very emotional and tore it into pieces. "You think it's that easy to get rid of me Lagant!" Her head was pounding harder; she went into the bathroom medicine cabinet for some Advil. She quickly took them and then called Lagant thinking, "What does he mean, we made a mistake? What is his problem?" His phone went to voicemail, *"Hi Lagant, this is Victoria; I'm calling about the note you left for me. We need to talk- call me when you get a chance ok, bye."* She sat on her bed feeling violated and confused.

Dirty Thoughts

It was a busy morning at McDonalds; Miss Cotton worked the drive thru. She saw a gold Acura pull up in line, through the monitor. She assumed it was Lagant, because the guy was flirting with her through the ordering panel. She had a big smile on her face; her smiled quickly erased when she realized it wasn't Lagant. She felt like they had a connection after the fact how he licked her up and down, she was able to see herself with Lagant; she liked how they talked and laughed about everything. She wanted to help turn the young prince into the perfect, strong King.

Lagant had her so horny that night, she had to finish what he started. She reached inside her toy box and pulled out her 9 inch vibrator, laid on the bed and started to tease herself. She let the vibrator work on her clitoris while she imagined Lagant eating her pussy. She opened her legs wider and let the dildo all the way up inside of her, "Yeah, baby I know you want my pussy, you got a chance to taste it." She was moaning and squirming around the bed gyrating it in and out. "Fuck your Queen's pussy!" Her juices flowed with every stroke; her body was so intense she could feel the fire in her soul. She grabbed the sheets and pulled them into a ball in her hand, "Oh my God!!! Kinggg!! Kinggg!!" She orgasmed like never before. The vibrator had hit her G Spot. After she finished she grabbed her pillow and drifted off to sleep dreaming about her King.

erica had planned on calling him when she got off of work but she couldn't wait so she called and left a message: *"How are you doing Lagant? You see I said your name correctly, don't need help anymore. But maybe you can help me with something else? I'll call you back when I get off, ok bye. Oh—I still have some of that red Alize left."*

The Tie In

Lagant was speeding down Shore Dr., his emotions had the best of him; he didn't know what to feel. If there was ever a time when he needed his father's advice, it was now, he didn't want his family to know that it was a possibility that Iesha wasn't his. His mind was scrambling. He turned the radio off; he couldn't stand to listen to another love song. Without him noticing, he ran a red light and the horns from the cross traffic brought him back to reality. He knew that he shouldn't have been driving in his state of mind. He decided to go to the beach, it always relaxed him.

The sound of the waves made him feel better; he watched the families lay peacefully on the beach. He went into a deep thought. He remembered what his shipmate, Lester, had told him about Jada when he first met her. Lester used to tell him—watch yourself with her; she seems to have some other hidden agenda. Lagant was young and didn't understand what Lester was talking about, he was just enjoying the fact that Jada brought and paid for everything. Now he was putting everything together; she was playing on his youth from the start. She started off by giving him lots of sex, money and gifts, the best a nineteen year old could ask for. But once she got him to fall in love with her, everything changed and the tables turned; she never wanted to go out any more, the gifts stopped coming and the sex slowed way down. He was now showering her with everything.

Lagant thought that he was the young player, now he realized Jada played him. But he never thought that she would be capable of cheating on him. He always looked at her as a mature woman who knew what she wanted in life; now he was learning a new side of her and her true colors. He knew he had to put his plan into effect and move out as soon as possible. He was happy that his brother was coming to visit. But the timing was all wrong. He didn't want his family to know about the drama that he and Jada were going through, so he decided to put the situation on hold until his brother returned home. Now he was hungry. He pulled out his phone and saw that he had four missed calls; he didn't know his phone was vibrating. He decided to have Calz pizza for lunch, he walked in and everyone working there knew of him from being a regular; they always delivered to his house. One of the delivery girls over heard him say that he was dining in; she was in the back ready to take her break and decided she would join him; she always would flirt with him when she delivered to his house. He would always give her a good tip; Jada used to notice their flirting and would come to the door rubbing her stomach.

Nicole Mosley was 20 years old. She worked at Calz part time and went to school at Norfolk State University. She resembled Beyonce but was a shorter version and one shade darker. Lagant sat down at the front table, "Can I join you", she said to him with her sunshine smile, Lagant was day dreaming, looking at the cars drive up and down the Blvd. "What's up Nicole? Yeah, of course you can." "How you been? I see you haven't been getting any deliveries lately?" "Oh—no, I had to give the greasy food a break." "I know that's right, you don't want to clog your arteries with all that cholesterol." "No, I don't—you right about that." This was their first real conversation; she always told herself that if she ever ran into him while he was by himself that she would approach him. "All this time I've delivered to your house, I don't even know your name?" "My name is Lagant." "Lagant—It's different—can I call you L?" "Why would you want to call me L?" "Plenty of reasons, you're always ordering large pizzas, your name starts with 'L' and it seem like you large and in charge—am I right?" (She was flirting and smiling) Now that she had his full attention, he asked, "Do you have a boyfriend?" "Yeah and no, it's nothing serious!" She remembered his girlfriend being pregnant, she asked, "Did your girl have the baby yet?" "Yes, a girl—her name is Iesha." She was waiting for him to say more and be more excited but he said nothing. She sensed that something was bothering him. "Are you ok?" "Yeah, I'm good—why you ask that?" "No, it just seems like you went into left field there—but congratulations on your daughter." "Thanks!" Nicole looked at her watch; her break was almost over, "Take my number and call me when you have some free time." He wasn't surprised at how straight forward she was, he stored her number. "Ok." She stood up and walked away, he watched and thought, "Girls just don't give a fuck!"

He sat there looking out the window; he couldn't eat his last slice. Nicole broke his thoughts by knocking on the window. She waved and signed with her hand for him to call her, and then she jumped into her green Cherokee. He thought about all the females that he was now involved with and remembered his Uncle Gene telling him, "Your life is a once in a life time deal; you better enjoy and take advantage of everything you can, while you can!" He thought to himself, "Fuck it—the more the merrier!" He jumped in his car and Big Daddy Kane's: "Ain't no Half Stepping" was playing. He took it as a sign that he had to step his game up.

Lagant picked up his phone and called Nicole, "what took you so long to call?" "Damn, it was only like five minutes!" "Hold on, that will be twenty two fifty—Hello?" "Yeah, I'm here." You could hear her breathing, running back to her jeep, "I wanted you to meet me but I don't know if I have time now." "Meet you where and for what?" "Come on, L—stop being scary—you don't have to worry about me telling your baby's mother anything." "Telling her what?" "That I'm feeling you." "She already knows that." "How?" "She said by the way you look at me when you deliver to us—I don't know—I guess its women's intuition— I see that she was right." She laughed, "What!—she couldn't see the way you were looking at me?" "How was I looking at you,—Nicole?" "The same damn way I was looking at you— lustfully!" "What about your boyfriend?" "What about him? I'm young and I know we're not going to last forever; he's doing his thing, we're both in college and our relationship isn't anything but a title— Besides, what he don't know cant' hurt!" (Gant thought to himself, all girls are secretive, slick and alike in one way or another, no matter what's their age!) "I feel you—where are you from?" "I'm from Maplewood N.J." "Oh you're from Dirty Jersey!—I'm from Newark!" "That's why I'm attracted to you—you from the hood—I like a rough neck!-are you a rough neck?" "You off the hook-I'm me!" "I'm saying—you from Newark and all—I could look and tell you have gangster in you—L—where you at?" "Sitting in my car in Calz's parking lot." "Don't go no—where, I'm coming down Virginia Beach Blvd—be there in three minutes." "Ok."

When she arrived she stood outside of his car leaning in the window while talking and flirting with him. The music was playing low out the car; she was dancing, moving her body, showing him what she was working with. In a kinky way her aggressiveness and confidence turned him on. One of her co-workers came to the door and called her, she had another delivery. She leaned in and gave him a kiss on the cheek and then wiped her lip gloss off of his face. "Can't have you going home with that on your face—I got to go, I'll call you! I know you'll be with your family just make sure you return my calls!" "You got that!" He pulled out of the parking lot and headed to the Moonlight, Nicole was on his mind as he drove. He knew he had to handle her tactfully; dealing with women; he had to develop a method of dealing with each of them accordingly. Maneuvering and sharing time with all of them would be a difficult task that he now had to master down to a science.

He needed a strong drink to sooth his nerves. every time he thought about his daughter, he envisioned Jada cheating. He figured he'd kill two birds with one stone: visit Star and down some drinks. He was at the light behind a green P&P van, he thought about Star's brother wearing the uniform the other night at the club. He guessed Shakur worked for them. He passed the van and two white men were riding. His phone started vibrating; it was erica (Buffy the Body) calling, "What's up my goddess?" "Hi handsome what are you doing?" "I'm headed to get me a drink." "It's too early for that!" "Yes, you're right but my baby's mother is driving me crazy!" "Oh, you have baby momma drama?" "Something like that—but nothing that a drink can't handle." "Did you get my message?" "No, I'm sorry I haven't checked my messages yet. What did I miss?" "Nothing, I was just thinking about you this morning and I called and left you a message." "My bad erica, I would've called you right back, I've been missing you ever since I left your house." "Oh really? {"Yes"} I miss you too, you had me open, I can't believe you almost had my cookies—I shouldn't have let it go that far." "erica don't fault yourself for being human, we're both attracted to each other—We are grown; what we do is between us, I'm not only interested in your sex—When the time is right—it will happen." She listened as her young King talked words of maturity, "So what do you expect from this?" Lagant was surprised that she asked that questions so soon, "Like I told you last night, I would like to be your friend and when it leads to anything deeper—then you could ask me that again." "I sure will!" She wasn't expecting that answer but she did respect it. "So what do you have planned for the day?" "I have to pick my brother up from the train station; if you like I could stop by and introduce you to him?" "What time?" "I'm waiting for him to call me now— but I'll call you before time." "Alright, make sure you call me!" "Okay gorgeous, I promise!" "I'll see you later handsome!"

He pulled into the Moonlights parking lot; he wanted to check his messages before he went into the bar. He smiled as he listened to Victoria's message; he knew she would call despite his note, which was part of his game. He wanted to see how much control he could gain over her. Next message was erica, he smiled as he thought about what she meant by—he could help her with something-. erica was a tease, he knew she had game and was willing to play her game until he scored. The next message was Jada saying that his brother had called, *"Your brother called he said he will arrive at eight o' clock tonight. I gave him your cell phone number— Gant, I don't want you to think that Iesha is not . . ."* He quickly hit erase before the message cold finish, the sound of her voice irked him.

As he walked to the bar he spotted the blood that was on the ground, "Damn!—it looks like he died out here." He walked pass Star's Land Cruiser and smiled as he reminisced about the night he drove it to Seafood Delight. It was a decent amount of people inside the bar; he took notice to the two ladies playing pool. He watched as the one lady bent over to line up with the q-ball, he liked the view from the back. He didn't want to get caught watching so he quickly turned his gazed, Star was busy working at the food bar, he went and sat right in front of her. Her back was turned calling in a food order, when she turned around she started smiling from ear to ear. "What's up baby?" He pointed at her, and then said, "You and me!" "You keep surprising me coming in here." "That's because it's somebody in here that I got attached too!"

Star was looking like a pink Barbie doll today with her hair in fluffy curls, a hot pink button up shirt that tied in the front right below her chess, with some pink shorts on. She looked tasty, the pink blended in with her completion. "I need a drink!" She looked at him with concern, "Hold up, what do you mean you 'need' a drink?" "You right baby—I want a drink." "Okay, that's more like it, let me buy you a drink what do you want?" "A double shot of Henny and a Corona." "Ok, I'll be right back with it, let me take this call."

He looked around the bar, the lady from the pool table was now at the jukebox; he liked her thick frame and bowlegs. As she turned around they made eye contact, she smiled and started walking his way. It was Lieutenant Washington who ran the personnel office at his job; he thought that body looked familiar. This was his first time seeing her in civilian clothes, she was more beautiful than he had ever imagined. As she got closer the more nervous he got, "Damn, she's coming right towards me."

He was about to stand up and salute her, until he thought about it, they were off duty and not in uniform. "Hello 'Ms.' Washington." She could tell that he was nervous, she smiled, "Sit down!" Ms. Washington knew that he had a crush on her, she always would catch him staring at her at work. "Relax Petty Officer Mills, we are not at work." She patted him on his back, "I guess I should call you Lagant— right?" He wondered how she knew his first name, they're not on first name basic and she pronounced it right. "I would tell you mine, but only on one condition, you have to promise that you won't tell anybody else." "That's no problem, my lips are sealed, Ma'am." "Oh please, cut the ma'am stuff out, I just told you we're not at work!" "Yes m' . . . I mean, ok." "My name is Gloria." "Gloria you have a pretty name." (He didn't know what else to say, he just listen and went from her vibe.) "Thanks Lagant. So, what brings you to the Moonlight?" "Oh, I just came out to get a drink and grab a bite to eat." He thought about Star, but he wasn't about to tell his long time crush about another woman. "I need a bite myself."

She sat at the stool next to him and waved the cashier over to place her order. He could smell Gloria's sweet smelling perfume; he looked her up and down, lusting after her. He was staring at the thickness of her thighs and how her ass swallowed the stool and how her breasts protruded through her blouse. He couldn't believe that he was actually sitting next to Ms. Washington at the bar. Lagant was trying to play it cool; the jukebox was playing Love & Happiness by Al Green. That was one of the songs she picked out. She looked at Lagant, "That's my song." She started singing along with the song, and she could really sing. Lagant smiled and bobbed his head to the beat, listening to Gloria sing; he was a sucker for a woman who could sing. She didn't have a drop of shyness in her; he sat there in a daze. Next song up was Minnie Ripperton's "Silly of Me"; the words of the song made him think about the love he had for Jada, which he felt made him a fool. He dropped his head in depression, she noticed and put her hand under his chin and lifted his head up. She handed him a napkin, "You ok Lagant?" "Yes, I'm okay, that song just always touches me." The waitress brought over Gloria's food and she started to eat, "Did you order yet?" "No, not yet, I was having my drink first."

Starlette brought over Lagant's drinks she saw Gloria singing and touching on him. She figured that she was trying to come on to him, "How much I owe you?" "It's on me, Boo!" Star cut her eyes over to Gloria to see her reaction, but she continued to eat with no expression. Star started to make small talk while he downed his drinks. "What was that?" Gloria asked while pointing at his drink, they answered her at the same time. "So, you just downed a double shot of Hennessey? You think you can do that again?" "Yeah—of course!" "excuse me, can you please bring me and the sailor man another one of those, please—thank you." Gloria only called Lagant that because she noticed the barmaid had a thing for him; Star looked at Gloria then at Lagant, "Sure, anything else?" "Yes, a Pepsi, thank you."

Starlette walked to the bar with her hands on her hips; she figured she had a little competition on her hands. She was used to having all of Lagant's attention. "Who's that—your girlfriend?" "She's a friend." "It seems to me she wants to be more than just a friend." Lagant smirked playing it cool; he sipped his beer. "You know that Hennessy is strong, can you handle it?" "We will see!" While Star made their drinks she looked over to the food bar. She didn't like the way they were interacting with each other, she was becoming jealous. When she came back with the drinks Lagant was laughing real hard, "What's so funny? I wanna laugh!" They both looked at her like she was an outsider, "Oh nothing, she just told a joke." "How much I owe you dear?" "$22.00" Gloria pulled twenty five dollars from her purse and said "Keep the change." She grabbed her drink and looked at Lagant, "You ready?" "Yeah!" She made a toast to the U.S.N., they held their shot glasses up, downed their drinks and banged the empty glasses on the bar when they were finished. "Wow!" Lagant chuckled, "You took it down like some champs!" Gloria put her hand on her chest, "It's burning going down." His eyes followed her hand and got stuck on her cleavage; he had to catch himself. "Chase it with your Pepsi!" He looked at Starlette; she had a blank look on her face. Gloria sensed the barmaid wasn't comfortable, so she extended her hand to introduce herself to Starlette, "Men are so rude. My name is Gloria." "I'm Starlette," she said with a half smile plastered on her face, "Nice to meet you, Starlette." "My fault, I meant to introduce you two." They both looked at Lagant and said "What—ever!" at the same time. "Starlette your hair looks nice—What shop did you go to?" "I did this myself but I go to Showtime's." "Oh, ok I heard about Showtime's. I have to check it out one day." "They all does good jobs, but I go to Kareema, she does it all-she's just the best."

Gloria knew exactly what to say to break her suspicion. They both talked and complimented each other on their appearances. Lagant listened and looked in admiration; he respected Lt. Washington even more. A tall slender young lady walked over calling Gloria's name, but she didn't hear her, she was too engaged in the conversation with Starlette. Lagant watched the tall slender woman approach; as she came closer he notices it was the lady who was playing pool with Gloria. She was better looking from a distance than up close. She tapped Gloria on her shoulder and looked at Starlette. "excuse me!" Starlette shook her head acknowledging her interruption; Gloria turned and said "What's up Linda?" "You're up next on the table." "You ready to lose again?" "Girl, you're the one on the sideline." "Come let me introduce you—Linda meet my friends, this is Lagant and his friend Starlette." They waved to each other, Linda was standing behind Gloria. Lagant was thinking that she wasn't a pretty sight but her body was out of this world. Gloria turned to Lagant, "Do you know how to play pool?" "Yeah—of course!" "You want to play? We could play teams? Starlette you don't mind do you?" "I do, but it's up to him." "Lagant, it's your call." Linda added her two cents, "Yes, come on, she's going to need the help!" Linda just wanted the young lamb in her circle so they could seduce him. "Thanks, ladies but I'm gonna have to take a rain check on the pool game." "You sure!—you going to let Gloria lose all by herself?"

Gloria laughed as she pushed Linda towards the pool table. They began to rack the balls up; what Lagant didn't know was that they liked to share. "He's cute—we could take him for a couple of rounds!" "He's enlisted, he works in my unit but in supply department; I can't chance it, he might have loose lips—But he will be discharged soon—I'll keep a tag on him." "I don't see anyone else in here that I'm interested in—it might just be you and me tonight." Gloria smiled as Linda winked her eye at her and licked her lips.

Starlette had a serious look on her face when Lagant turned his focus back to her, "You okay Star?" "Yes I'm okay—I'm wondering if you're okay, I see you can't take your eyes off of her ass! Don't you see it enough at work?" He grinned; he knew she was jealous, "Star, she's a co-worker, that's all!" "Are you sure? Because I can see straight through her—she wants to be more that a damn co-worker!" In the back of his mine he hoped she was right, {females could always tell.} "Star I don't have anytime for any other woman; do you really think that I want to mess up what I have with you?" With that statement she felt a little more comfortable. (She was letting what her brother said to her about service men take hold on her.) "I just don't know about you Navy guys!" "No Star, not you too!" "What do you mean—not me too?" "So what—every guy that's in the Navy is a whore? That's what you mean—right?" "Right!" He looked her in the eyes, he could see this was about to be an argument something he don't need right now. He stood out of the stool, pulled a twenty out of his pocket and placed it on the bar. "What is that for—I don't want your money" "I don't want you to pay for this whore's drinks-I'm out!" "Take your money back!"

He ignored her as he walked out the door; Linda tapped Gloria when she saw him stand up at the bar. They could tell that there was a dispute, they watched as Star ran out of the door after him. Star realized that she was wrong for comparing him to the rumors that she heard and knew about Navy men. "He must have that platinum!" "Girl, we'll find out in do time." "Girl I hope soon; I want some of that platinum plus shit to make me chase like that."

Starlette caught Lagant as he was pulling out of his parking spot; he turned down his radio and rolled down the window. "I'm sorry baby, I didn't mean it!" He got out of the car; she jumped into his arms and looked him in the eyes, "Do you forgive me?" He pulled her closer, "Of course I do baby!" "Don't leave yet, please!" "I don't want to baby, but I have to pick up my brother from the train station in an hour." A blank look overcame her, "What's wrong?" "I wanted to invite you over my house for the night; I was looking forward to rewarding you for your bravery the other night!" Lagant was now smiling, "Well, then what's stopping you?" "You want to stay the night with me?" "Hells yeah!" "Good, meet me back here when you're finished with you brother." "I could meet you at your house—just give me the address." "I could do that but I have to work late, I'm covering for my brother tonight, he's coming in late." "Okay, I'll meet you here then—I'll call you when I get here." "Okay baby—it sounds like a plan, don't let me down." "I won't!" She smiled and threw her arms around his neck, "Give me a kiss" They tongue kissed passionately, "Okay, now you can go!"

Starlette felt special as she walked back inside the club, she felt him watching her walk away. He was happy that everything had worked out, he didn't want to lose Star from his newly formed harem, and she was his favorite. He jumped in his car heading to the train station; he grabbed his cell phone and called erica. "Hello." "You still miss me?" "No not really." He pulled the phone away from his ear to make sure he had the right number. "That's to bad baby because I miss you like I missed church on Sunday." She paused, and thought about it for a second, "So is that a good miss or a bad miss?" "I'll let you answer that. Do you like church?" "How are you going to answer a question, with a question?" "easy—you hold the answer." "So what if I say no—I don't like church?" "Then that's your answer." "So that means you don't miss me?" "You said it not me." "Hold on— erica come and get this phone, it's your young prince." Lagant was listening to the background, "Girl you have a live one, he thought I was you and said something about miss you like church then he used reverse psychology on me." "Tiffany what are you talking about?" "Hello Lagant." She knew it was him because no other men called her house except her son's father, and she wasn't expecting Shakur's call until Sunday when he return their son. "I hear that I'm your prince?" "Tiffany told you that?" "No, I just over heard her telling you that." "Oh, don't pay her any mind, that's my crazy ass friend." "Girl I'm not the one who is crazy—when he really gets to know you—he'll know whom the crazy one is!" "Do you hear her Lagant? Tiffany, girl watch the movie and not me!" "Your girlfriend had me fooled I thought she was you." "What's this church stuff she's talking about?" "That's not about much; I'll let her tell you—I want to know more about being your young prince? You know I like power, what do I have to do to be your young King?" "It's a lot that comes with that position, first I have to learn a little more about you and make sure you're not promiscuous. You may have a bunch girls running around behind you, But, don't take this the wrong way; you're too young to be crowned my king—you must be willing, ready and able to protect me at all times—King comes with a lot of responsibility." "I'm bout that—the question is you ready to be my queen?" "You not ready boo" "Well ok you win—would you still like to meet my brother?" "Yes of course, nothing has changed." "Okay good, his train comes in at eight. I'll call you back when we're on our way." ""Sounds good, make sure you call me back my prince." She chuckled. "I will your majesty!" "erica, it sounds like you really like him." "I do but he's still young and I don't want to be the one to destroy his innocence." "You're right, you know—he's never going to be crowned your King unless you're willing to wait another 13 years for him—This is what you do!— let him know that you want to keep it on a casual basis and call him up when you need your back broke." They shared a laugh, "Girl, your right! I was ready to try and turn him into something he's not ready for! But he's so fine—and those sexy ass lips!" "You've been single too damn long! Just let him scratch that itch and that's that! You better not crown that young nigga king." Tiffany started watching the movie again while erica grabbed the throw pillow and hugged it against her body thinking about her young prince.

As Lagant put his cell phone on the seat he heard a car horn; he looked over and it was a blue convertible BMW with four white girls smiling and waving. They sped past him on the highway; he didn't know them from a can of paint. He looked down at his speedometer and was doing 70 mph. So they had to be doing 80+ mph. He reached into the glove compartment, grabbed his NASCAR gloves and slid them on. Keeping an eye on the BMW, he down shifted into fourth gear, he could feel the car engine pulling for power. He quickly shifted back into fifth gear and watched as the speedometer reached 90 mph. He was creeping up fast on the BMW, when he got beside them he blew his horn. They looked over at him, "There's the guy in the gold Accord!" They waved and smiled as their hair blew in the wind, Lagant signaled for them to show their breasts. The blond in the front and the brunette in the back seat both pulled up their shirts, exposing their breasts. He gave them the thumbs up; the BMW sped up cutting him off as they exited the highway. She blew the horn and they all waved goodbye.

He realized Virginia is really the place for lovers. His cell phone was ringing, he picked it up, and it read wifey. "I have to change that!—What's up, Jada?" "I'm just calling to see if you're on your way to get your brother?" "Yeah—Why—did he call you back?" "No, but I know you left out of here upset and when I called you didn't answer, so I just wanted to make sure you got my message." "Yeah, I got it." "I'm frying some chicken and I made the other bed for Khalil. Gant, we need to talk! "She was so shook up she didn't know how to get to the point. "I'm listening." "I don't want to talk over the phone!" "Jada, I need to know if that baby belongs to me! I'm taking a DNA test!" "I thought you said you heard my message; I set up the appointment, it's for Wednesday at nine in the morning — But I know that Iesha is yours!" "How you know Jada, you fucking cheated on me!" Jada replied very low with a voice filled with sorrow, "He wore protection." He could hear her sniffling, "Who the fuck is 'he' Jada!" "I don't want to talk about it over the phone." "Just tell me-believe me it's better for the both of us talking over the phone,—is it anybody that I know?" "Gant it doesn't matter."

Lagant hit the end button, he wasn't going to play the run around game with Jada, and he wanted answers. "Fucking bitch!" He pulled into the train station and parked as close as he could to the front door. He stood outside his car and waited for the train to pull in. He looked around at all the other people waiting for their friends and family, people of all colors and nationalities. His cell phone started to vibrate. He sighed, as he reached for it thinking it was Jada calling back, but to his surprise it was Victoria. With his hectic day it slipped his mind to call her back, he knew he had to get his player skills up, —its hard being a player, but it sure is fun!— "I'm sorry I didn't call you back, my day has been very crazy!" "Is everything okay?" "Yeah, it's nothing I can't handle." "Lagant I'm not trying to add on to your hectic day but I need to understand why you think we made a mistake?" Victoria was straight to the point she wanted answers, Lagant already had what he was going to say to her planned. "Ms. Parker you were my baby's mother's nurse, I don't know but I started to feel guilty." "Lagant we talked about that—I thought I understood your situation—you told me that she was only your daughter's mother—Are you two trying to make things work out?" "No!" "Then why you don't want me calling you anymore?" "Miss Parker . . ." She interrupted him before he could finish, "Lagant why are you calling me by my last name?" "I don't know I just feel that it's appropriate." "So last night meant nothing to you?" "Yes! It was one of the best times of my life!" "So then it's appropriate that you call me Victoria!" "You're right, I apologize." "Lagant I'm going to cut through the chase; do you still feel you made a mistake with me?" "No, not at all—I had time to think about it. But the only thing that concerns me is . . . I just don't want any problems!" "Lagant I told you I'm not going to cause you and Jada any problems!" "Victoria you say that now, but if you keep operating on me like you did, don't you think that feelings are going to get involved?" "I'm not going to lie to you, my feelings are already involved. If they weren't I would have never slept with you—The thing is I'm a big girl, I know how to control my feelings—Let me know if you don't want to be bothered with me anymore?" There was a pause between both of them, "how could I not be bothered with the best RN in the world!" "I hope not, I wouldn't want you to go back on your word!" "What word are you talking about?" "You promised me that you would take care of your pussy!" "Oh, no I wouldn't want to go back on my word—How is my pussy?" "She's a little sore." "Want me to kiss it?" "I thought that you'd never ask." "Didn't I promise to take care of her?" "Yes—yes you did!" Victoria was happy that she could keep a hold on her Black Knight; they both were laughing and flirting. "How far do you live from the train station?" "Less than ten minutes; why you ask that?" "I'm out here now, waiting for my brother, he's coming up from New Jersey—If you're not doing anything stop by so you can meet him." "Okay I can do that, let me turn off my pot roast." "Oh you cooked, is it done yet?" "Yes it's done; I just had it on low keeping it warm—Would you like some?" "Hell yeah!" "Okay, I'll cut enough for you and your brother and I'll be on my way." "Sounds good, I'm not rushing you but try to hurry baby, his train should be here soon." "Okay baby!"

Victoria cut the roast, grabbed her keys and headed to the train station to meet her Black Knight. Lagant leaned on the hood of his car browsing through his phone. He counted his four new numbers and stored them under Star, Cotton, Park, and Cold. He figured Nicole was coldhearted; as he thought about how loose she was. He knew he had to school the college girl on some things if they were ever going to work out. Soon as he cleared the screen, it vibrated and Cold appeared on it. He thought that he had made a mistake and called her. He decided to have a little funny with her. "What's up Calz pizza?" "Don't call me that! You know my damn name!" "Can I have a slice?" "You're going to stop playing with me!" "I was just looking at your number." "Stop lying, why you didn't call me then?" "I didn't know if you were with your boyfriend." "What does he have to do with you calling me!" "I didn't want to get you smack around or into any trouble." "Trouble, I'm grown, he doesn't own me!" "Oh okay, I feel you ma!" "If anything you're the one that would get into trouble, you have the live in!" "I'm the man; I don't get in trouble." "Oh yeah, you the man? Then meet me on Princess Ann Ave. at the 7/11." "Why are you trying to test me?" "You the man right; it shouldn't be a problem, am I right?" "I would but I'm in Newport News right now, at the train station waiting to pick up my brother." "Oh okay, how long is he staying?" "I don't know—as long as he wants." "So, I should get a chance to meet him then?" "Why you want to meet my brother?" "I don't know—I know you're going to always be with him showing him the town." "When I meet up with you it's just going to be me and you—feel me ma!" Lagant started walking to the ticket station, it was five minutes passed eight; he looked at the schedule and realized that the train was delayed by fifteen minutes. "Okay, so just you and me?" "Yeah, just you and me, you're not scared are you?" "Scared of what?" "Scared of me!" "Please!" "Okay—so when I ask you for a slice, you already know what it is!" "A slice of what?—A slice could be many things, I wouldn't know what you are talking about." "I just have to show you what I'm talking about." "I guess so." Lagant was letting her know in so many words that it was just going to be a fuck thing with them; he shifted the conversation. "You just got off work?" "Yes, I got off at eight." "So you were trying to see a nigga after work?" "Yes—but your ass is a whole hour away, it's Saturday and I'm not ready to go to my dorm." "I see

135

you like living dangerously." "I need some excitement in my life!" "Don't worry you've met the right man! excitement is my middle name!"

They talked until he heard the train coming; he was putting his Mack down on her, molding and positioning her to fit into his newly found world. He told her that he would call her back after he got his brother situated. When the train pulled in and everyone exited, Lagant spotted his brother easily. Shit, he stood at 6'4"; he was at the tail end of the train. Lagant got excited like the rest of the crowd waiting on their arrivals. He bumped into people as he walked towards his brother yelling his name. Khalil heard his named being called and spotted his little brother coming through the crowd; Lagant saw that his brother now had a bald head with a full beard trimmed low, it fit him. Lagant gave him a bear hug, and grabbed one of his bags. "How was the ride?" "Long as hell! I met this fine lady though, she's a teacher at Chesapeake high, where is that?" "It's not to far, the next city over, it's like 30 minutes away." "Ok, her name is Kerrine, I got her number. She wants me to call her tomorrow when she gets out of church. I told her I was Muslim and that she was too, from birth; that's how the conversation really started. I gave her a drink of the juice and she was all ears! I got her—she's super hooked!" "You know mom raised us in church, how you give up on your first love?" Khalil's face became serious, "Little bro, we've been deceived by the bible's teaching, they twisted a lot of the truth!" Lagant pressed the trunk button on his alarm, "Where's your Audi 5000?" "I traded it for this." Lagant placed the bags in the trunk while Khalil inspected the car, "Bro, I like this!" He looked at the chrome rims, "What're those, 22's?" "No, they're 18's." They both started laughing. Lagant repeated him; "you said 22's" and continue to laugh. "I know you be pulling a lot of honeys with your pimped out ride?" "No—I be doing the pimping!" "Jada gonna fuck you up!—"Shit, they say Virginia is for lovers"—"but Jada got you on lock—you're a father now." "Yeah that's true!-but Jada ain't got shit on lock—I have a couple of honeys on my team. You're going to meet my nurse any minute, then we're going to make a quick stop in Portsmouth and I'll let you meet my Buffy the Body!" Lagant was smiling and popping his collar as he bragged to his brother. He told him all about the Latino mommy that Jada sent to test his loyalty. "Bro, usually when a girl does that she feels guilty about her own loyalty to you. Her conscience is bothering her and she just wants to get some dirt on you! What did the mommie tell Jada?" Lagant thought about what his brother was saying, and he was right, missing pieces of the puzzle. He wanted to tell him the whole Jada story but first he wanted to find out if Iesha was his. "You alright, bro?" "So what did the mommie tell Jada?" "She told her that I passed; she couldn't tell her that we fucked, they work together. I smashed a few more times at her place, until she stated feeling guilty— Shit, I told her I was still trying to pass the test!" They both laughed as his phone began to ring. "Pardon 'self, this is my nurse." "You here baby?" He looked at the entrance of the parking lot and saw her BMW pulling in. "Yes, I just turned in, where you at?" He gave her their location, "Where she at, bro?" He looked up and saw the BMW pulling up behind them. "Damn bro, she got that paper!" Victoria stepped out of the S.U.V and Khalil was star struck, he thought she was Vida Guerra the model. He used to collect all of her posters from magazines when he was in prison; get money to them, (in other words-masturbate). Victoria hugged and kissed Lagant. She stood there looking naturally beautiful while he introduced her to his brother. Khalil stood there staring at her hair being tossed by the breeze; he had a flashback of prison. She extended her hand, "Hello!" Her voice brought him back to reality, "My bad, you remind me of someone, nice to meet you!" Victoria walked to the passenger side of her S.U.V, "I brought you guys some of my pot-roast, I hope you like it." She handed the container to Lagant, he opened it and the aroma hit his nose, "It smells good!" He grabbed a piece then passed it to his brother. "It tastes good!" She looked at Khalil, "I know you're hungry after that long ride—enjoy!" "Yeah, that train's food is garbage! But this roast smells great, with the gravy and potatoes . . . ! Thanks, it's right on time!" "You're welcome!" Khalil couldn't help himself, "Do you have any pretty girlfriends like yourself that you can introduce me to?" "I'll tell you what, once you're all settled in, I will have a dinner party and you can take it from there!" She smiled with her arms wrapped around Lagant, looking at the both of them. "You would do that for me?" "Yes! Why not, you're Lagant's brother." Lagant just stood there smiling; she was making him feel important. "Ok, that sounds like a good idea, let my brother know and we're there!" "Okay." "Thanks again for the food!" Khalil walked to the passenger side and got into the car while Lagant walked Victoria to her S.U.V, "You've done a good deed today!" She looked at him with her hazel eyes, "I made collard greens and rolls; if you like, you two can come over and get the complete meal." (This girl would do anything for me.) "I would love to but my brother is already complaining about a shower; I know he's ready to relax." "I understand!" He stepped closer and rubbed her shoulder, "Thank you for coming through on such short notice." He started giving her small kisses that led up to a big tongue kiss; he dropped his hand to her ass and palmed her cheeks. A guy about five cars back yelled out, "Get a room!" They laughed and Lagant gave him the middle finger, Victoria broke away. "You better cut it out before I kidnap you! — Go ahead and take your brother home and call me when you can—okay?!"

Lagant jumped in the car, "Damn, lil bro, she's fine as hell! Did you smash that yet?" "Just last night—she took care of a nigga!" "She looks like Vida Guerra?" "Oh yeah? pass the roast bro." Khalil passed the container with one piece left. "Damn, your ass is still greedy as hell!" "A nigga was hungry after that ride; that shit tasted good as hell!" Lagant just looked and shook his head; they hit the highway heading to Portsmouth. "Bro we've got to go food shopping tomorrow. You're not eating me out of house and home!" They both started laughing, "You think my nurse is bad, wait until you see erica! And don't be lusting all over my girls either, you have to get your own!" "Nigga, you married with children, you can't be trying to lock'em all down—they're open season!" "Married! — you don't see a ring on my finger, I'm about to stick a fork in Jada—she's done!" "You buggin, that's your baby's mother, plus ya'll got over three years in together. That girl loves you and I know you love her!"

Lagant just drove looking straight ahead with a blank look on his face; he could feel Khalil looking through him. "You do love her, right?" "Bro, what's love got to do with it?" "She is your daughter's mother! —you don't want her raised by no other nigga, do you? — You fuck these other girls but you keep family first! Don't split your family up unless it's a 'real' cause!— You're my brother and trust me; I won't tell you nothing wrong; if you can work it out, do that. Fuck these other bitches!—nurse and all! Feel me?" Lagant still wasn't ready to open up to his brother, he just listened. "Yeah bro, I feel you, I'll take the fork out of her." He just said that to make him feel good and stop talking about it; if he knew the real reason, he would have stuck the fork in her back his damn self; he switched the conversation. "My boo, Star, I feel a special connection with her, she's cool as hell. She wants me to spend the night." "Tonight? How're you going to leave me on my first night down here?" "You're going to be alright, I know you tired anyway—tomorrow is another day then we're going to ride out." "When do you go back to work?" "I'm on leave for 2 weeks, so I have enough time to show you around." "That's what's up. How Jada doing?" "She's good; they gave her a month off to get settled, she's frying some chicken for you."

Khalil knew that something wasn't right between those two, but he left it as it was; he figured all couples went through their ups and downs. "How does it feel, being a new father?" The question made him think about the diary; he didn't know how to answer that one. So, he said what he thought to be the normal answer—"It feels good, she's so pretty and innocent." Just thinking about it made him upset that it was a possibility the baby wasn't his. He tried to hide it but Khalil could tell that he was uncomfortable. He knew being a father for the first time was the most proud feeling a man could have and his brother wasn't showing any excitement. "Little bro, what's going on with you and Jada? We're blood brothers, there's not suppose to be any secrets between us!" "The bitch cheated!—she cheated on me and Iesha may not be mine!" "Oh shit! Are you sure—how do you know?" "I read it in her diary,—fucking—trifling ass—BITCH!" Khalil thought back to their earlier conversation and now everything made sense; he couldn't believe it; Khalil thought that Jada was one in a million—a good girl. When they would come visit him in prison, she seemed to be loyal and had her mind right; she had the family thinking highly of her. They knew she loved him from the things she did for Lagant. Khalil was far from being a fool; he knew that life was full of twist and turns. But this was a major problem. "Calm down bro, you're speeding; I feel your pain— that's why you said she was done. But let me ask you, what if the baby is yours?" "I will take care of her and love her but I just can't fuck with Jada like that— it's over between us!" "What's she saying about it?" "She says that Iesha is mine—that she used a rubber with whoever it is that she fucked— She won't even tell me who it was; she's probably still fucking him and they laughing in my face." "How long have you known?" "I just found out last night—that's not it bro—I also found out in the delivery room that she had a son!" Khalil's eyes got wide, "A son! Jada has a son? Where is he at?" "She put him up for adoption when she was a teenager." "Wow! —Wow!—yeah! — Now I see why you're out here whoring around town, but bro, that's not you. And it don't make it right either." "The funny thing about it is they all know about Jada." "It doesn't matter, playing girls could be dangerous—think about it—Do they know each other? What if one of them gets pregnant? Woman are emotional beings when they catch feelings; do you think you're going to be able to just cut'em off? I'm just saying be careful—you're a good man and I don't want to see you get caught up in anything! Remember two wrongs don't make a right." "I understand, but it makes me feel better!" "It might help you feel better for now, that's only temporary. You still have a lot of growing and learning to do!" "That's the same thing erica told me earlier— That's who we're going to see now; I came close to smashing that last night—she got a fatty!" "How old is she?" "She's 31." "You like older women, huh? You need a girl around your age—older women will try to mold you into someone that they want you to be—either that or they just want some young buck dick." "I don't have a problem with that!" "Look, you still thinking with the wrong head." "Bro I got to get mines—I tried that loyalty stuff" Khalil just laughed, "I feel you player." He knew his little brother had to learn life and become a man through his own life experiences.

They both grew up without their father being around mainly Lagant and with Khalil being the older one; he did his best to advise him without breaking their brotherly bond. Lagant was at a red light; he had decided to take the back streets, he made a right turn while Khalil was rolling up a bag of sour diesel. He sparked the blunt and rolled down the window halfway, "What—you trying to get me kicked out of the service?" "This little bit of smoke is not going to do anything to you." "That shit stinks!" "It's supposed to—dis dat sour!"

Khalil was enjoying the sights of the new city, he leaned his seat all the way back and turned the music up. Lagant was thinking about everything they had just talked about and he concluded with, "let the dice roll, it is what it is, I have to do what makes me happy." While stopped at a stop sign, he noticed that green P&P van parked mid-way up the block. As he passed the van he saw Shakur standing outside on the side walk in his work uniform with three other guys that were roughing him up, pushing him up the driveway into the house. He watched through his rear view mirror as he passed; it was dust dark but his senses picked up on everything. As he approached the next stop sign he knew that he had to do something to help Shakur or Starlette was going to have a dead brother. He made a quick right and parked, "Is this where erica lives?" Lagant placed his head on the steering wheel debating with his self. "Bro, what's wrong?" "Did you see that green van back there?" "Yeah, what about it?" "That's my girl Star's brother, I saw three guys just push him into that house; two of them had guns." "Your girl Star's brother! What! You better call the fuckin cops and let them do their job!" "Bro, by the time they get here he's going to be dead!" "So what the fuck we supposed to do? I'm not playing super hero, especially for a nigga I don't even know!" "I know bro, I'm going to handle it." "You fucking crazy you think I'm about to let you go in there and get killed? Gant them niggas have guns, they will kill your ass! Call the damn cops like I said."

Lagant hit the button to his stash box and pulled out his .380 and the Glock 9 automatic. Khalil was shocked to see his brother pulling out the guns, but he was more upset than anything. "What the fuck you doing riding around out here with guns in the car? You got beef with somebody?" "Nah, bro I'm down here all by myself—I have to protect my self. I don't want to get caught slipping!" "Nigga, don't you know that you can get ten years if you get caught with them shits!" "That's what I have a stash box for, they'd never find them!" "Bro, I don't know what you got going on down here, but I came down here to get away from that type of shit!" "Bro, you don't have to do anything—like I said I'll handle it."

There was a brief moment of hush; Khalil was looking at his brother with disbelief. Never did he imagine his little brother shooting out. This was what he tried to keep him away from; he knew that you could take the man out of the hood but not the hood out of the man. "Bro, I'm not letting you go in there alone. If you get hurt mom will think I came down here and got you into some shit! So how you want to do this shit?"

Lagant started to strategize, putting his entire military tactic to use; Khalil grabbed the nine and cocked it back. "Fuck that shit bro, we going in here and ain't taking no prisoners. That shit you talking might work if you came to arrest a motherfucker; but not in no street hit. This shit right here is for keeps—this is real life! You want mom to hear on the news that both of her sons got killed in a shootout? I don't give a fuck how many people in there—we have to shoot to kill, we go in, get your man and we out! Straight like that!" Lagant looked a little spooked, he thought about what his brother was saying, but he didn't want to kill anybody. He just wanted to stop the guys from killing Shakur, but he knew that his brother was right about this being real life. "You sure you want to do this?" Gant looked, gripped the .380, "Yeah bro, I feel it's the right thing to do!"

The three men had Shakur sitting in a chair putting duct tape around his hands and feet. One guy had a gun pointed at his head; Money Mel pulled a chair up facing Shakur. "I only have one question to ask you— but before I ask—I want you to think about something before you answer— think about your pretty little wife and children—think about your gorgeous little sister—If you don't co-operate with me my goons will have lots of fun with them bitches—Oh—and don't think I forgot about your son's mother, erica, she not too far from here—right?"

we go way back, you know I would've done anything you asked of me—Why are you doing this?" Shakur spoke humbly while Mel blew smoke from his cigar into his face; after he let Shakur finish talking, he put the cigar out on his leg. Shakur screamed out like a bitch; the big guy punched Shakur in the jaw and he spit out blood. "Mel, please you don't have to do this!" "It's too late Shakur; you've been getting fat for along time now, you think I don't know? You're a fucking—millionaire! You should have been cut me in, but you want to be greedy. You don't know how to step to the side and let another motherfucker get a piece of the pie! So now I'm just going to take mine!" Shakur began to panic and plead, "Mel, let me give you what I got—and we can forget all about this!" "Forget!?!" Mel grabbed Shakur by his curly hair and yanked his head up. "You think I buy that bullshit, hustler?! It's over son—you had your run, just think about it this way, your family will be good. You're kids will grow up and have a great future."

Shakur knew that Mel was going to kill him after he told him where the stash house was. But he also knew it was the only way to save his family. He was in a lose-lose situation. "Are you ready to answer the six million dollar question?" Mel cocked his gun and put it into Shakur's mouth, his eyes beamed directly into Shakur's eyes. Mel's eyes got smaller and they turned red. "What's it going to be—life —or death? Choose wisely?" Three tears dropped from Shakur's eyes, Mel took the gun out of his mouth. "Life!" Rushed out his mouth. "Good answer—let's get it! You're doing the right thing for your family. We're going to put you in the van and you're going to give us the directions to your stash house. And if you lie about anything, I'll keep you alive just long enough to watch while your family dies one by one, starting with your kids!" Mel told his goons to put him in the van; the big guy gagged Shakur's mouth and lifted him across his shoulders.

Lagant and Khalil had crept up and were peeking through the windows. Once he saw the guys tuck their guns, Khalil whispered, "Now!" Khalil gently opened the door. Mel saw the door open up but before he could reach for his gun Khalil let off one shot hitting him directly in his chest. Money Mel flew backward crashing against the wall. His man Tarik yelled out, "What the fuck!" He tried to reach for his gun but it was too late; Lagant was down on one knee already aimed at his chest. He let off two shots from the .380 and Tarik stumbled backward slowly, falling to his knees. He looked down at the blood that was leaking from his chest; his face had the shocked look of death. Blood spilled out from the corner of his mouth then he fell forward on his face. Shakur didn't know what was talking place; he just heard the shots, making him even more scared. He didn't like cops but tonight he was praying that it was them, he'd rather go to jail for cocaine charges and stay alive, than to be murdered for it.

Khalil had the Glock 9 pointed at the big guy who still had Shakur over his shoulder. His free hand was in the air waving that he wanted to surrender. Khalil waved his gun motioning, telling him to put Shakur down. "Put him the fuck down! And don't try any stupid shit!" He slowly put Shakur down and then stood up, Khalil yelled, "Put your hands on your head and get on your knees." He did exactly as he was told, Lagant patted him down and pulled a .45 Smith & Wesson from his waist and kicked him onto the floor. Lagant slid the .45 to Khalil, pulled out his blade and cut the tape off of Shakur.

Once Shakur saw Lagant's face, he thought that he was dreaming. He didn't know why or how he was there to save him. But he was thankful and happier than a fag in prison to see Lagant, out of all people. Lagant gave Shakur the .380, "his fate is in your hands." Lagant grabbed a towel off the table while Khalil yelled out. "Hurry up!" The big guy was pleading for his life, "Please don't Shakur; it was Money's crazy ass idea please!" Pop—Pop—Pop! Shakur let off one to his head and two went into his chest. "No mercy, you bitch-ass nigga!" "Let's go!"

Khalil was already half way down the street, Shakur jumped in his van while Lagant wiped down any finger prints they may have left. He jumped into the van with Shakur and told him to make a right at the corner. Shakur couldn't stop thanking Lagant, "Please—meet me at the club tonight!" "I'll be there!" Lagant jumped in the passenger's side of his car, Shakur hauled ass in the van. You could hear the tires skid as he turned the corner. Khalil pulled off nice and easy like nothing ever happened, Lagant heard his phone going off, it was erica; he sent the call to voicemail. Khalil looked at him while resparking his Dutchmaster. "That was erica, you got to meet her another day, we have to get the fuck out of Portsmouth. Make that right onto the highway." Khalil was looking at Gant, smiling and pulling on the weed, he said. "I didn't know you had it in you, lil bro! You got good aim too—you did this type of shit before?—you wiping prints off and shit,— you watching too much TV!" They both started laughing, "Hell yeah I wiped shit down, I don't want either of us doing life in prison. Feel me?" "What's up with your like he had seen a ghost; he wants us to meet him at the club." They drove and talked about the situation, Khalil put him up on the tricks and trades of the murder game, and how the cop's played dirty to scare you. He let him know—you must not open your mouth about this to anyone, not even Jada; not your best friend; not even yourself. "After we talk to your man this chapter is closed!" Lagant nodded his head in agreement; he told Khalil to take the next exit and, at the Hotel 8, turn left and drive to the back of the parking lot. Hotel 8 had a dock over the ocean. When they reached the back of the parking lot; Khalil noticed how nice the view was. The moon reflected over the ocean, he could see all the way to the horizon. "Give me the Glock bro." "For what?" "I'm about to get rid of it." "Bro we don't throw away guns!" "We can get more guns!—That's a murder weapon, I took that gun from somebody—we don't know what's on that gun." Khalil didn't want to part with it, but he knew his brother was right. "What you want mom to read that her sons are in prison for a triple murder? Man, give me that gun!" Gant grabbed it, broke it down then wiped it off, wrapped it up in the towel and put it in a bag and tossed it into the water. "Where's the .380?" "Shakur has it; I hope that he got rid of it!"

Lagant took the wheel; they were off to the Moonlight. He pulled in the back of the club and parked. Lagant was out of the car when he saw Khalil tuck the .45 in his waist. "What you doing bro?" "Gant I don't know what you got going on down here; I've been here less than an hour and I have a homicide and am an accessory to two murders. I don't know what the hell we walking into now, I don't trust these niggas down here! Shit, all I wanted to do was meet my new niece and relax." "Bro, I'm sorry I got you tied up in this bullshit, just chill in the car, I'll be right back." "Nigga we blood—you go, I go—and the gun goes too! I told you in this murder game you can't get caught slipping—your gun is your bitch!" "But it's a bouncer at the door." "Fuck them bouncers they're not cops. The rules change in the murder game—There ain't no rules—you make your own rules! Listen, your bitch works here, use your pull and get us in." "Yeah, you right!" "I know I'm right, the Navy got you slipping."

They walked to the front door, the bouncer noticed Lagant, "Follow me, Shakur is waiting for you." He opened the door and they followed him into the back of the club, they looked like VIP status to the watching eyes. Lagant looked around for Star but didn't see her, the bouncer knocked on the office door and Star opened it. She immediately hugged Lagant as tight as she could, "Baby I was worried are you okay? Thank you for saving my brother s life, you're an angel! This must be your brother?" She hugged

Khalil and thanked him; Shakur was standing up behind his desk, Khalil took notice of the .45 on the desk. "Come in, come in!" Star locked the door and Khalil spoke up, "nice gun." "It's the twin to the one Lagant took off of Deebo, he had took it from me." Shakur had a huge knot on the side of his forehead and his top lip was split and swollen. "Lagant I owe you and your brother my life for what you both did for me. You not only saved my life, you saved the lives' of my family; if there's anything that I can do for you two—and I mean anything—let me know!" Lagant gave Star a look of curiosity. "I'm not trying to pry into your business Shakur, but why did those guys want to kill you and your family."

Shakur looked at Star, making them look at her and she nodded to Shakur assuring him. "Shakur you can trust them to know; they just saved your life!" With that he told them everything from his legit business to his cocaine business, {all Khalil thought about was this being his big payday. This was the connect that he needed to lock down up top (think about Newark).} Shakur continued. "I just thank God that you two showed up!" Shakur paused and looked at Lagant, "You are a mysterious man, first the car, now out of nowhere you're on time to save my life—I'm forever grateful but I can't understand how it's possible." Lagant kept it short and simple; he couldn't let it be known that he was going to see another female. "Yeah, you don't only have my brother and me to thank, you have to give God the glory. I was just picking my brother up from the train station and decided to stop in Portsmouth to visit one of my dudes when I saw your van and then I saw them pushing you up the drive way—I knew you needed help. And on the strength of your sister we gave you a helping hand—You might want to thank your sister!" Shakur came from behind his desk and hugged Lagant and Khalil, "I can thank you enough!" He looked at Khalil, "With all this crazy shit I never introduced myself properly—I'm Shakur, I know that your Lagant's brother but I need to know the man who helped save my life!" "Khalil!" (They shook hands) "Thank you Khalil, I know what you did was on the strength of your brother—but I want to show the both of you my appreciation—I hope that half a mill' a piece will accommodate you? But like I said—anything and I mean anything I could do just let me know!"

Lagant couldn't speak, he looked at his brother; and thought I know he didn't just say he going to give me a half of mill' all he could see was the green-dollar signs never in his wildest dreams he thought saving Star's brother life would bring him a start of an fortune. Khalil remained calm, paying close attention to every word Shakur had to say, he picked up on his key words; like when Shakur said **HOPE & ANYTHING**. Khalil answer, in street judgments "That will do—but I need to discuss somethings with you when you get yourself together." Shakur figured what time it was, he had been in the drug business long enough. Shakur replied, "Yeah, sure—can you both meet here at 11am tomorrow? I'll have everything ready for you." Lagant was still looking spaced out; "We'll be here" Khalil spoke up.

Lagant never had that much money at one time; he was already spending some of it in his mind. First thing he thought of buying was a big house, Star didn't like the look that was on Gant's face, and she thought with that much money he would forget about her. Shakur pushed the .45 on his desk, "Take it, they're twins—they need to stay together. The .380 is in the ocean, the only people who know anything are in this room and the tree dead people in Portsmouth and that's how it's going to stay!

{They all looked around at each other and then nodded in agreement.} Well guys, I'm going to take care of some thing's, if you need me for anything let Star know and she'll contact me."

Shakur hugged them all again before leaving out the back door. He sat in his van and looked at the paint bucket with the 10 keys in it. Then he noticed the duffle bag that Money Mel had brought with the $200,000. "He tried to rob me and 'I' came up— thanks to Lagant and his brother." Shakur knew that this was 'the sign' that Sam used to always talk about; passing the pie; it was time for him to retire. He knew that Lagant would be the perfect candidate; he was young and reminded him of himself in so many ways. He admired his heart, he liked how he moved, he knew that Lagant had the makings of being a young boss and he figured, if any man could get his sister to say that she loved him, that man had to be intelligent. Shakur knew that Khalil would have Lagant's back and he was prepared to teach them everything that he knew. Shakur was going to introduce Lagant to the official members and pass his position down when the time was right. He thought it over in his mind. "Lagant is the one! When I'm finish training him he'll be one of the best young bosses and hustlers around! I'll call him Kato cause he remind me of the Green Hornet." Shakur was good for giving his best men nicknames on how he see their inner personality

Planting Seeds

It was quiet in the office after Shakur left out; Lagant sat down in Shakur's black plush leather chair that was behind the desk. Starlette knew that her feelings for Lagant grew too fast but it felt so right to her. And what he did to help her brother made her feelings even stronger. She just hoped that he wouldn't put her on the back burner now that he had money; she knew how money can change a man. Khalil sat on the desk thinking about locking the streets of Newark down and turning his half of a million into multi-millions. Now he was starting to hate the fact that he was on the run, he knew that to be successful with his plan he had to turn himself in.

Lagant felt his phone vibrating, it was freaky ass Nicole—he sent it to voicemail, and he saw that he had 20 missed calls and 12 messages. He sat in the chair rocking from side to side with his mind drifting off he couldn't believe he was going to have a half of mill' in his hands by tomorrow the murders was already off his mind his mind was on the money to what he would do with his half of a million. He was going to move his mother out of the hood into a big house and buy her a new car, and then he was buying himself a brand new car; he thought of the 745BMW. Then he wanted to open a Go-Go bar and name it Get'em Girls, he was trying to map it all out. Khalil peeped that Starlette was in deep thought, he broke the silence. "So you're the Star that my brother is head over heels for." She smiled from ear to ear, she was happy to hear that statement; she walked over to Lagant and kissed him on the lips. "I'm head over the heels for him too! He's my Boo!"

Lagant sat there with a smile on his face listening to them talk and become more acquainted with each other. Khalil could tell that she was a little shook and spooked by her brother's close call. He was speaking word of encouragement, letting her know that everything was going to be alright. Lagant was sitting back in the boss' chair listening to his message; he felt like a King listening to his harem of women leaving message after message it was like they were howling for him. Starlette made eye contact with him then winked her eye at him and continued talking with Khalil. At that moment Lagant realized to himself that he had player status & boss status was on its way soon. Soon as that money touches his hands it's was off to the races. He knew now, what he always thought about when he was younger, growing up as a young teen—in the hood that life was about Sex, Money & Murder!!!!

TO BE CONTINUED . . .

Born and raised in Newark, N.J. after graduated from West Side High school, joining the Navy for nine years, attending Desert Storm and Desert Shield, being honorably discharge 1997, pursuing my first love, rap artist, teamed up with A-reel ent. Branch off to do my own becoming C.e.O. of Black Panther ent. Kato production, being new to the industry and exploring different avenues along with my up's and my downs! I returned to my home town. Being over qualified for most job positions and now along with an felony. I pursued what I was natural born to be an entrepreneur.